The Secret
of the Blue Trunk

The Secret
of the Blue Trunk

LISE DION

Translated by Liedewy Hawke

DUNDURN
TORONTO

Editor: Shannon Whibbs
Design: Jesse Hooper
Printer: Webcom

Library and Archives Canada Cataloguing in Publication

Dion, Lise
[Secret du coffre bleu. English]
    The secret of the blue trunk : a novel / by Lise Dion ; translated by Liedewy Hawke.

Translation of: Le secret du coffre bleu.
Also issued in electronic format.
ISBN 978-1-4597-0451-0

    1. Martel, Armande--Fiction. I. Hawke, Liedewy II. Title III. Title: Secret du coffre bleu. English.

PS8607.I6434S4213 2012   C843'.6   C2012-904315-X

1   2   3   4   5   17   16   15   14   13

We acknowledge the support of the **Canada Council for the Arts** and the **Ontario Arts Council** for
our publishing program. We also acknowledge the financial support of the **Government of Canada**
through the **Canada Book Fund** and **Livres Canada Books**, and the **Government of Ontario** through
the **Ontario Book Publishing Tax Credit** and the **Ontario Media Development Corporation**.

We acknowledge the financial support of the **Government of Canada**, through the **National
Translation Program for Book Publishing** for our translation activities.

Care has been taken to trace the ownership of copyright material used in this book. The author
and the publisher welcome any information enabling them to rectify any references or credits in
subsequent editions.

J. Kirk Howard, President

Front cover photograph and interior photographs: author's archives.

Printed and bound in Canada.
www.dundurn.com

Dundurn	Gazelle Book Services Limited	Dundurn
3 Church Street, Suite 500	White Cross Mills	2250 Military Road
Toronto, Ontario, Canada	High Town, Lancaster, England	Tonawanda, NY
M5E 1M2	LA1 4XS	U.S.A. 14150

To the two wonderful grandchildren of a grandmother who was a survivor. They have also played an important part in their mother's survival.

To Claudie and Hugo, so that you will always remember.

Author's Note

I have intentionally changed the names of certain people and places out of respect for those who have lived through that unthinkable killing frenzy, in particular for my mother.

The Discovery

For two days I had been trying to get hold of my mother by telephone. But she never answered. Although I knew she was often out, I was worried. I called the superintendent of her building and asked him to check if she was home. I wanted to be reassured at all costs. "No problem," he said. "I'll call you back in fifteen minutes."

Half an hour later, he still hadn't called back. I was sick with worry, like a mother who can't find her child. Finally, after forty minutes, the telephone rang. The superintendent asked me to come immediately, but I wanted to know before I left if my mother was all right or if she was ill. He repeated urgently, "Come right away!"

On the way over, I imagined the worst. I pictured her lying on the floor, flat on her stomach. She was trying to drag herself to the phone to call me and ask me to help her. I felt sick, distraught, I couldn't stop crying, and barely managed to keep my mind on the road.

When I drove up to her building, I saw police and paramedics bustling about. I don't have a clear recollection of what happened next. I remember the superintendent hugging me to stop me from going inside. Choosing his words with infinite care, he explained that my mother had been dead for several hours. It was better for me not to see her in that condition.

A fellow tenant who lived on the same floor as my mother and knew her well invited me in while I waited for the father of my children to arrive and to take control of the situation because I was unable to.

Then a policeman and a paramedic came to reassure me. They explained that my mother had died of a pulmonary embolism and had already lost consciousness at the moment of her death. When they entered her apartment, she was simply sitting in her armchair. So she hadn't had time to try to call me, as I had pictured in my mind.

Their explanations made me feel better. They also told me there was no indication whatsoever that she had suffered before she died. I was relieved. But when they mentioned that her death might have occurred two days earlier, a tremendous feeling of guilt overcame me. And that feeling haunts me to this day.

A few hours later, morgue employees took my mother's body away. Only then could I bring myself to go into her apartment.

The first thing I caught sight of was her nightgown. It lay on the floor near the chair in which she died. I shrank back. It was too much for me. I asked the superintendent and my husband to get rid of any traces that might remind me of my mother's last moments.

When I finally stepped into her small furnished place, a strong smell of decomposition hit me. It was a distinctive odour. Even if you've never smelled it before, something tells you it is the smell of death. It's like the scent of cheap face powder that turns your stomach, but at the same time there's the stench of something cold decaying.

I thought I would never be able to get rid of that smell. It clung to my nostrils and my clothes. But worse were the fathomless silence and the great emptiness pervading her apartment. My only thought was: I must gather together all the necessary documents as quickly as possible and get out of here.

When I think back on the days I spent at the funeral parlour, I realize I was in a trance. All I wanted to do was sit on the floor and cry my eyes out. Yet I struggled to keep calm. I must have been afraid my behaviour might seem a little excessive because of my grief, but we all mourn in our own way.

Before they closed the casket, I wanted to make sure my mother had everything she needed for her great journey. I lifted the satin cloth covering her body and checked if they had put on the wool socks I had brought. My mother always had cold feet. I would have liked to wrap her in a warm blanket but restrained myself.

To me, my mother was still alive. It hadn't sunk in that all life had left her body. This lasted a few hours. That's why I insisted she wear her glasses. I wanted her to be able to recognize the people waiting for her on the other side, should there be another side.

My children and I put all kinds of objects in her last bed. My children gave her drawings and wrote her affectionate notes, whereas I wrote her a long letter in which I asked her among other things to send me a sign from time to time. Especially when I needed her advice.

Around her, in the casket, we placed a few pictures of Maurice, her husband, and of their marriage. Maurice was the love of her life and, according to her wish, she would be buried by his side. Next to her, near her head, we placed a photo of her beloved brother Rosaire.

I also laid a few *Salix iona* stems in the casket. They were her favourite flowers, members of the willow family. She called them simply her "little pussycats." Every summer, she would search high and low for them, gathering them into bouquets.

My children and I wanted her to take along all her familiar things. It was our way of delaying the final closing of the casket. The funeral director didn't seem too happy about our activities and kept giving us odd looks, but we just couldn't resign ourselves to seeing her leave forever.

At the cemetery, I noticed there was water at the bottom of the grave. I became hysterical, I started screaming that the casket wasn't watertight, that the water could seep into it. I even asked that they pump that water out before lowering my mother's casket.

The gravediggers, who had seen worse, didn't budge, and forced us to leave before they proceeded with the burial. My children thought I had been acting rather strangely since my mother's death. I think I scared them a little. They were eleven and thirteen and had never seen me in such a state.

❖ ❖ ❖

Barely twenty-four hours after my mother's funeral, the superintendent of the building where she had lived notified me that the apartment urgently needed to be "cleared out." Apparently, a new tenant was eager to move in.

"Cleared out," he said. What a dreadful, coarse expression! He was trying to make it plain to me that life went on and a mere coat of paint would get rid of any trace of the admirable woman she had been.

I almost shouted at him, "You can't possibly have known her well, or you would be mourning her death and not pressing me to throw out her soul!" When we experience great sorrow, other people's everyday concerns become intolerable to us.

I plucked up whatever courage I had left and could at last bring myself to open the door to her home. If I had gone there with brothers and sisters, I think it would have been easier. Even though I know that often in large families people quarrel over an insignificant scrap of fabric that isn't listed in the will, I found it very difficult not to be able to share these dramatic moments with anyone.

When I went in, the smell of death was still just as noticeable. I opened the windows to air out the place. Inside, everything was stagnant, as if time had stood still since she died. After a quick survey, I realized that the task would be very hard: In a few short hours, I needed to get rid forever of all traces of her presence in these rooms where she had lived for nearly eight years.

Before I began, I sat down on her bed. I felt utterly bewildered. I stroked the blankets, which still held the imprint of her body.

I wondered how I would manage to live without her. Although I was thirty-seven years old, I was still her child, a child who had suddenly lost the security, the consolation, and the sympathetic ear of her adored mother. Never again would there be someone looking at me as if I were still a little girl and say, "When you were small, you were like *this*, you delighted in doing *that*, your father and I loved you so much," and so on. Never again would I be able to take refuge with her.

Whenever I visited her and she was in the kitchen preparing a meal, I felt as though I were coming home from school and was a child again who no longer had to face her adult responsibilities. No matter what problems I discussed with her, she always found solutions or gave me advice on how to deal with them. Of course, we had our disagreements, but how sweet it was to make peace with each other afterwards.

With tear-filled eyes I searched every nook and cranny of her bedroom. Her perfume still had the place of honour on her dresser. I opened the bottle and threw a few drops into the air to make the room smell good, as if to tell myself that she was still there. "I'll use it sparingly," I thought, "a little daub once in a while, on days when I'm depressed, to make myself feel better." Also on her dresser stood her beige, gold-patterned, leather jewellery box. As a little girl, and even as a teenager, I used to spend hours emptying it and playing with her jewellery, carefully examining the pieces one by one. Then I would put them gently back in the velvet-lined compartments. I discovered, hidden in a corner, two baby teeth of mine she had kept. I couldn't help bursting into tears. A splendid photograph of my father was prominently displayed on the desk. In that photo he looks steadily at the camera with a loving smile. My mother and I always found that smile irresistible. My father had remained ever present in my mother's life, though she survived him by twenty-seven years. She often said she would never again live such a love story. That's why she had chosen to stay on her own.

Very early on, I realized that my parents formed a special couple. When my bedtime came around, for example, they became two childless adults again. It was out of the question that I would disturb their privacy. Yet I certainly tried. My parents were ahead of their time. In the first place, my mother, Armande, was ten years older than my father. Secondly, they lived together for several years before getting married, which wasn't done in those days. It created a scandal in the family.

They shared a tremendously strong bond and talked to each other a lot. That, too, was rare in those days. I so much would have liked her to tell me more about that great love affair, to help me understand why she broke down so completely when my father died.

Still sitting on her bed, my mind adrift, I pictured my mother walking into the bedroom to take her nap, as she did every afternoon. I so much would have liked to lie down beside her and take her in my arms for that final rest. I would have thanked her, then, for her generosity of spirit and, especially, for her extreme unselfishness to have looked after a child of which she wasn't even the biological mother.

I would have liked to thank her once more for all those hours she spent hunched over her sewing machine making clothes for people who were better off, not to mention the housecleaning she did in private homes, so that the widow she had become too soon could make ends meet.

I would have wanted to tell her, too, how grateful I was for all the sacrifices she made for me. How many times did she offer me half of her meal, pretending she wasn't hungry anymore, so I could eat my fill?

She also tightened her belt to be able to afford presents for me at Christmastime. I remember a ring she once gave me. She'd bought it on credit, paying five dollars a week for it. I've never been able to part from that ring and wore it until it practically fell to pieces.

And more than anything else, I would have wanted to say to her, "Don't worry, Mom, I'm here, I'll stay with you until you close your eyes. I'll hold your hand until you see that beautiful light they promise us, and until the hand of the one you loved so much takes over from mine ..."

I just couldn't make up my mind to pack up the objects in her bedroom. I was so overwhelmed with grief, all I did was cry.

Finally I decided to start with the kitchen. I didn't feel like lingering, it was too difficult. There was no more time to waste, anyway, because the people from her neighbourhood to whom I wanted to give her things would be arriving in a few hours. I am sure my mother would have agreed with that.

On the table I spotted her handbag and slowly emptied it of its contents. I hated doing this; it was like accepting that my mother was gone for good. Much to my surprise and half-laughing, half crying, I found things she had stolen from me. Over the past few years I've often been the victim of her little burglaries. Thus I retrieved, from a small pocket, my silver earrings, which I thought I'd lost, and a multicoloured glass pendant that caught her eye whenever I wore it. While sorting clothes in her chest of drawers, I actually found a sweater, a nightgown, and even a pair of shoes that belonged to me.

In her wallet I discovered an old picture of the two of us, taken in a photo booth during Expo 67. I was twelve. We were both laughing. I started crying again. My mother's smile was joyful. There was nothing forced about it, as in an official photograph.

I can honestly say that my mother and I had a wonderful relationship, although sometimes she would have liked to have me all to herself, and then sparks flew. Strangely enough, we began to feel very close to each other when I was a teenager, but that bond was, in fact, an expression of her possessiveness. She was jealous of the time I spent with my friends.

My mother also had a fiercely protective side. She could easily have become violent if someone had tried to attack me. Whenever I was sad, she moved heaven and earth to cheer me up. I remember how one day, when she couldn't bear to see me cry over my weight problems anymore, she suggested we buy a miracle product that could make me lose weight. But the sale of that product was illegal in Quebec. So she was capable of putting aside her integrity to find a solution to my distress. On the other hand, she had a strong tendency to bear grudges. I dreaded her fits of rage more than anything. When she was angry at me, days could go by without her speaking to me. I detested that because, after my father died, there were just the two of us in the house. Her silence and indifference would quickly become intolerable.

Most of the time, though, we were happy together. We liked good food and were eager for new discoveries, which she always initiated. We went to Expo every weekend, for example. We didn't have much money, but by bus or metro we were able to visit Montreal from east to west, north to south.

On Sundays we sometimes went to the Central Station, just to savour the atmosphere and watch the travellers. She was passionately fond of travelling, but we couldn't afford to take the train. So we would go to the station to dream.

Having a deep love for French culture, she introduced me to French cinema. I got to know all the great actors and actresses. Sometimes I stayed away from school, with her consent, of course, and she would take me to department stores like Eaton's, Morgan's, and Dupuis Frères. She taught me how to be elegant and put out-fits together, always with good taste. She also taught me to tell a high-quality perfume from an inferior one. To her, having no money did not mean looking shabby. It was always possible, even necessary, to dress properly and look smart. That's how she taught me good manners. My mother had class. She loved chic, stylish clothes, jewellery, and fine-leather shoes, but since she couldn't afford them, she made do with visits to stores. She had no compunction about fingering lovely fabrics on dummies, and would closely examine the cut and seams of a piece that appealed to her so that she could draw the pattern and make the garment herself at home. She also stressed that clothes should last a long time.

Shoes were another aesthetic preoccupation of hers. When she tried on a pair she liked, she would parade back and forth in front of the saleswoman with an undecided look on her face. Only my mother and I knew that those shoes were yet another daydream. She would come home delighted by what she'd seen and quickly forget about all the things she'd hankered after, and be happy with what she had.

Toward the end of her life, when we visited a store, she occasionally stole a few small things without my knowledge. She only showed them to me once we were outside. In this way she stole sunglasses, a Barbie doll for my daughter, and tools she had absolutely no use for. At one time she filched a screwdriver just for its beautiful blue plastic handle. I didn't know what to do with an eighty-year-old shoplifter. No doubt I should have gone back to the store and asked to speak to the manager, and then make her hand over her haul. But I really didn't want to be ashamed of my mother. I much preferred being her accomplice.

In her kitchen, there were lots of Chinese dishes to pack up. That's understandable. We often went to the Chinese quarter for a meal. My mother thought nothing could top that. One of her friends, who was better off than she was, took her out for a meal at a restaurant once in a while. Armande invariably chose Chinatown. It would be a memorable occasion, and we'd put on our Sunday best. When I taste Chinese food, I can't help thinking of her.

Once the kitchen was empty, I went back to the bedroom. Sobbing, I stripped her bed and breathed in the smell of her sheets one last time.

Now all that remained to be emptied out were the contents of the big blue trunk. The mysterious, unfathomable, untouchable blue trunk, which intrigued me throughout my childhood because it was always locked. Opening it was forbidden under penalty of severe punishment. As a little girl, I didn't even dare imagine the kind of sanctions she might have inflicted on me.

Timidly I approached the trunk, with the key I'd found at the bottom of her handbag, in a small velvet pouch that also contained a statuette of the Virgin Mary.

I was afraid I'd hear her tell me off. Slowly I lifted the big lid. The silence was oppressive, but no reprimand broke it. The smell of naphthalene wafted up. That was probably the best remedy against moths turning my christening gown into Gruyère.

There were boxes containing my childhood mementoes, several photographs, some of my father at a military camp. I didn't know he had done his military service. And there were pictures of my mother taken by my father. In one, she stands near a boat. In another, she sits on the fuselage of a plane, and yet another shows her leaning on a car, smoking a cigarette. These pictures expressed the tremendous love he felt for my mother and were further proof of the deep bond between them, especially when she looked straight at the camera.

O r d o n n a n c e

Vous devez vous considérer a partir de ce moment
comme detenue. Vous ne devez plus quitter vôtre
appartement, on viendra vous chercher. Vous devez
emporter des vêtements chauds.
Toute tentative de se soustraire a cette ordonnance
entrainera la peine de mort.

     Rennes le 5.12.1940

Mme. Amande Martel
Mlle.
31 rue d'Antrain

R e n n e s   Der Kreiskommandant
             I.V.

            H a u p t m a n n .

The order for Armande Martel's arrest, issued at Rennes, Brittany, on December 5, 1940.

There were also a few mementoes of my stay at the orphanage. One photo showed me in the company of a nurse who had a loving look in her eyes. I was smiling at her. These photos must have been taken on the day Armande and Maurice came to get me. My mother kept my official adoption papers in that trunk, as well. I had never seen them before. They gave the date of my departure from the Crèche d'Youville, April 1956, seven months after my birth. I knew I had been adopted, but I didn't think I had spent so much time in that institution.

At the bottom of the trunk was a medium-sized black box. Inside it were several holy pictures, a velvet case containing a black rosary, quite worn out by the hands that had used it, a dog-eared missal of the same colour, medals of various saints, St. Joseph and St. Christopher among them, and a great many pictures and statuettes of the Virgin Mary.

At the bottom of the box I discovered a photograph of my mother with her brother Rosaire. She wore a nun's habit! I couldn't believe my eyes. Yet it definitely was my mother: I recognized her in spite of her young age! There it was, no doubt, her great secret ... but there were other secrets the box would soon surrender to me. Papers, written in German, stated she was under arrest. I was totally baffled and could barely concentrate as I struggled to decipher the writing on all those yellowed papers. One of them commanded my mother to obey orders under penalty of death.

I had plunged into another universe, that of the Second World War. Many questions rushed into my mind. I couldn't find suitable answers to them for the moment. How could my mother have been involved in that conflict? I had always thought that her life had on the whole been rather quiet.

Like everyone else, I had heard about that inhuman war. I knew about the atrocities committed, but the thought that my own mother might have been caught up in the insanity shattered me. Could it be that my mother was a victim of the Second World War? The papers definitely referred to Armande Martel, my adoptive mother. They furnished evidence of her arrest by the Germans at Rennes, in Brittany …

I immediately asked myself: Was my mother Jewish? And what was she doing in Brittany? According to her certificate of baptism, she was born in Chicoutimi, on April 6, 1912. Fortunately, there were other documents in the box. They might provide answers to my questions about her being in Europe.

Now my mother transformed into a real heroine, a central figure in the conflict. I pictured her as a defiant prisoner who had somehow turned into a Resistance fighter. I knew she had the backbone to come out of the war alive.

At the bottom of the trunk I discovered something else: a bulky envelope containing five hardback notebooks tied together with a white ribbon yellowed with time. On all five notebooks my mother had written the same title: *So that I will always remember.*

She had enclosed a letter with the notebooks, which was addressed to me.

My dearest Lise,

If this letter is in your hands, it's because I am no longer here, since, while I was alive, you weren't allowed to touch the blue trunk. You must have opened the box I put on top of the envelope containing the notebooks, and found the two passports without pictures. I tore those pictures out myself, to prevent you from discovering certain things.

I concealed part of my life from your father, particularly my years in the religious life. I wanted to keep those secret. When he died, I decided to tell you my story through these notebooks so you would know after my death what my life was like. I am leaving you my secrets, which, I hope, will help you to understand the way I acted now and then.

I wonder where I found the strength to go through all that I tell you in these pages ...

I want you to know that I love you and wish you'll be able to manage in this life, which can be so harsh. Seize every chance to be happy! That's what I wish most of all.

Please don't weep for my past when you read my story, I already have. I will always watch over you, dearest Lise.

Mom

I was stunned and knew even before I began reading these notebooks that my mother had left me an exceptional story.

Finding them gave me the necessary energy and inner peace to finish the task I had set for myself: to distribute all her possessions. At last I could inscribe the words "The End" on her life. As for her other life, the one filled with secrets, I took it with me, in that blue trunk. It was a priceless inheritance, a treasure I was eager to discover.

I moved the big, blue, metallic trunk with the brass corners to my home and put it in my bedroom. It looked impressive at the foot of my bed. I knew I would never part with it because it held the essence of my mother's life, which had just begun to reveal itself to me.

I started to read that very evening. I unplugged everything that might ring, closed the curtains, and bolted the doors. I couldn't wait to begin and didn't even bother to create an atmosphere conducive to reading. I stayed cut off from the outside world for two days.

When I opened the trunk, I had a sudden dizzy spell at the thought of what I was about to find out. As I lifted the veil from my mother's hidden life, I prepared myself for an unforgettable experience.

I always looked upon my mother as an ordinary working woman who lived modestly. She had to come home at night, tired out from her day. I thought she was caught up in a boring routine. More than once I quizzed her about her past, but she always found a thousand and one ways to evade my questions. Now I knew she had things to hide …

Since she asked me to, I want to make this incredible story public.

Armande will be our guide, thanks to her notebooks. I hope you will find them interesting!

We'll meet up again later.

First Notebook

Childhood

For my dearest Lise,

As far back as I can remember, I have always kept a diary. Writing has brought me much comfort. It has allowed me to express my joys, and my anger, too. It also caused my downfall, since I couldn't help describing what was happening around me.

Let's begin at the beginning, with my grandparents. My father, Onésime Martel, was the son of a farmer. He lived in the parish of Saint-Wilbrod, at Hébertville-Station, in the Lac Saint-Jean area. In June 1908, he married the village schoolteacher, my mother, Virginie Martel.

A year later the two of them settled in the Bassin Quarter of Chicoutimi. This was essentially an industrial town, where, on the Chicoutimi River, two pulp-and-paper mills were built, which grew into the largest businesses in the Saguenay region.

My father was hired by one of those mills. Actually, there were a great many construction sites; there was plenty of work in the town. The company built houses for its employees to live in with their families. My parents rented one of these. They were small wooden dwellings, all constructed to the same design. So we would recognize ours, my mother had put a wooden crate painted blue on the porch.

I was born in the parish of Sacré-Coeur on April 6, 1912, three years after my brother Armand, the family's first child, who only lived for a few months. I don't know the cause of his premature death, but my mother's grief must have been immense, since she called me Armande. A third child was born, Rosaire, then a girl, who also died shortly after birth. Then, in 1918, another brother, Louis-Georges, arrived. Mom died of the Spanish flu a couple of months after his birth. She was thirty-three, I was six. I remember that her health deteriorated in the space of a few hours. She seemed perfectly fine, and then, the next moment, she was in bed, sweating profusely, coughing, unable to breath normally. She died two days later.

My father was devastated. He cried a great deal. He was in such despair that he seemed to have forgotten about us. His one concern was to stop us from playing outside because of the epidemic. Since most of the people around us thought that everyone was infected, no one went outside.

I recall seeing our neighbours leaving on stretchers. In fact, all the members of one family went to the hospital like that and were never seen again.

People covered their mouths with masks and we were very scared. I remember that my brothers, Rosaire, four years old, and Louis-Georges, six months, cried constantly.

Alice, my father's sister, took care of us. My father had nicknamed her "the Crow" because of her jet black hair. She looked extremely stern, which frightened me.

When she arrived at our place, she was terrified of catching the virus, so she wore a piece of cloth in front of her face and would only touch the baby. She was nearly always in a bad mood and chronically impatient. She made sure we knew we were a chore for her. Needless to say, I didn't like her.

I was heartbroken by my mother's death and cried a lot. Aunt Alice did nothing to comfort me. Not once did she give us a consoling hug. I missed my mother's caresses. I had been the child she had longed for, the one who had survived, the apple of her eye.

One evening after supper, Alice announced to her brother that she no longer had the strength to bring us up since she already had three children of her own. She agreed to look after my two brothers because her two daughters, who were older, could mind them, but caring for me was out of the question. My father didn't know what to do. There was no one else in the family who could look after us. Alice suggested he should place me in the orphanage run by the Augustinian nuns de la Miséricorde de Jésus. She gave him a week to make a decision.

Being just six years old, I was incapable of looking after my brothers. My aunt had tried to teach me housekeeping, but I was much too young to cook the meals and take care of the children while my father was working. The only thing I knew how to do was soothe the youngest one when he cried so Alice wouldn't get annoyed. My father worked six days a week. We hardly ever saw him anymore. It's at this time that he started drinking after work. When he came home at night, we were already in bed.

So, what was meant to happen happened. A few days after Alice spoke to my father about the orphanage, she woke me up earlier than usual while letting the others sleep. She bathed me, washed my hair, and dressed me in clean clothes. During this ceremonial, she talked to me in an emotionless voice. She told me I had to go and live somewhere else for a while, and from now on I would be looked after by nuns.

"Those women are the brides of the Baby Jesus," she said, "the very one you pray to every evening for your mom. They take care of sick people and children who have lost their parents. For you, it will be like going to school, but you'll sleep there at night so you'll get to the classroom earlier." She painted a detailed picture of what my life at the convent would be like, praising the good meals I was going to have and the friends I would make. To ease her conscience, she tried to convince me that I should consider myself lucky to be given a new life where I'd be able to get an education, since even her own children wouldn't have that chance.

I remember I wasn't terribly excited about the plan. To begin with, I had no idea what she was talking about because I had never seen a nun. Jesus was just a man with a beard in a picture on the kitchen wall, in front of which Mom asked us to kneel every night without ever really explaining who he was. Besides, I knew nothing about school, since no one around me had ever gone there. I sensed something didn't ring true in her speech because, while she explained things, she never dared look me in the eye. She ended her monologue by telling me that my going away was temporary. I didn't know then that I would never set foot in her house again, nor in mine for that matter. When I'd had my breakfast, my father came to get me and took me to the orphanage.

When I caught sight of the huge grey building, I became very afraid. My father had to pick me up and carry me in his arms because I wouldn't take another step. I clung to his neck so tightly he could barely breathe. I thought that the closer I clutched him, the harder it would be to tear me from his arms. I sensed that something serious was afoot.

When we went inside the big building, the first thing that struck me was the smell of floor polish and disinfectant. It made me feel sick. We were shown into an office to meet Mother Superior. My father tried to explain why he had decided to send me to this institution, but I understood from his words that my aunt didn't want me anymore. This confirmed that Alice hated me. I felt a deep sadness welling up inside me and, above all, an immense feeling of abandonment.

When he got up to shake the nun's hand, I began to scream and vomited my breakfast onto the floor. After wiping my mouth with his handkerchief, my father wanted to kiss me before he left. I threw myself at his feet, gripping his leg. He couldn't move, and I wouldn't let go for anything, like a drowning person clinging to a buoy.

Mother Superior shook a bell and Sister Marguerite appeared at once to give her a helping hand. The nun succeeded in detaching my arms from my father's leg while she spoke to me softly and stroked the nape of my neck. My father was crying, too. He finally left without looking back.

Sister Marguerite took me to a small parlour so my cries wouldn't draw everyone in that part of the building toward us. While I still rolled around on the floor, gentle Sister Marguerite kneeled down beside me, stroking my hair all the while. She already knew I had quite a temper.

After a few minutes, her reassuring voice managed to calm me down. I had never felt so safe since my mother died. I let her cradle me in her arms, and we both sat like that until my grief faded.

Then my new friend showed me around the convent. I held her hand very tightly. I was impressed by the high ceilings. The windowless doors of varnished wood seemed impenetrable to me.

After climbing stairs and walking down corridors, we arrived at another huge door. The nun opened it. When I saw what was in front of me, I froze. An enormous crucifix hung on the white wall. Lined up below it were about thirty metal beds. Beside each bed stood a chair and a bowl for washing. At the back of the huge dormitory, behind a white curtain, one could make out a narrow room with a bigger bed, for the supervising sister.

Sister Marguerite knew I had lost my mother and she was obviously trying to comfort me, especially after my father had left me in her hands. She rummaged around in a cupboard and gave me an old doll, which must have belonged to a former boarder, to break the loneliness I had been plunged into lately. She explained to me that my mother was in heaven now, and this doll could sleep with me and would help me be less sad. I clasped that doll in my arms as if it were the most important thing in my life.

Then I put it down, with my bundle of clothes, under the bed she assigned to me, and we continued going around the premises. I obediently followed this woman who had been able to gain my confidence and was making a funny noise with her long black robe as she walked.

The bell rang for the midday meal. Right then began for me the first day of a boring daily routine that would last about twenty years.

Every morning, the wake-up bell rang at half past five. We had to make our beds straight away in silence, walking with bare feet on the ice-cold floor.

Next, we slipped into our black uniform, topped by a white collar. Before washing ourselves, we had to kneel at the end of our bed and pray. Quite often I needed to use the chamber pot under my bed because I couldn't control myself. All the girls would see me and, especially, hear the noise I made as I urinated. Needless to say their taunts were awfully humiliating. But the voice of the nun always called them to order: "Silence, young ladies, and hurry up!" I heard this sentence so often that after a few months I no longer took any notice of it.

After that, we headed with our earthenware basin for a room at the very back of the dormitory to wash ourselves. We only washed from the waist up and it was forbidden to take off our camisoles. We had to wipe our bodies with a linen face cloth without ever looking at ourselves or looking at the girls next to us. The soaked, icy camisoles would take an hour to dry on our bodies.

We then had to attend Mass and receive Communion. Afterwards, we were allowed to have breakfast, which was a cold, pasty gruel.

Then classes started. I was eager to learn. Looking at books, touching them, seeing pictures, discovering figures, using a pencil: it was all new to me. I rarely felt sad on school days. Time passed quickly and I didn't really have the opportunity to think about anything else.

Before the evening meal there was a study period. At supper, we were almost invariably served a vegetable stew with half a slice of bread. During the meal, a nun would read excerpts from Biblical texts, and then came the vespers ceremony. There was no doubt about it: our life already resembled that of the nuns. We went to bed at half past seven, not before a final study period.

As time went by, the convent became a comforting cocoon for me, and the religious community became my family.

At first I had some difficulty with the discipline. I was a rebel through and through and didn't always do what was expected of me. I often demanded to be given the reason why it was my duty to perform some chore or other. At those times, Sister Marguerite came to my rescue and tried to calm me down. I was so anxious not to disappoint her that the mere mention of her name would make me toe the line. But altogether I was a good student, with an enormous desire to learn, despite my hot little temper …

I made some good friends, who shared my daily life until our teenage years. Several left the convent then because they were old enough to help out at home. I felt a pang of sorrow whenever a friend left. And I couldn't help thinking of my family. Since the day my father had consigned me to the nuns' care, he had only come to see me once, for barely fifteen minutes, and his breath reeked of alcohol. He told me how my brothers were doing, whom I hadn't seen since I left home. My father's visit disturbed me profoundly. I was twelve, and I remember feeling tremendously angry. I accused my father of being nothing but a weakling. He hadn't been able to face up to his responsibilities and defy my aunt. Why had my brothers, but not I, been allowed to remain part of the family? It was terribly unfair.

I ended up deciding I didn't want to have any more visits from my father, since he opened a wound that was slow to heal after he left. Whenever I felt homesick for my family, I talked about it with Sister Marguerite, who would listen to me and explain certain things. I was able to go to sleep then, my mind at ease until the next time.

My teenage years were obviously peaceful. I performed all the tasks required of me. I was taught housekeeping, cooking, and sewing, the nuns' way, which meant with diligence and perfection. I was a quick learner. I had a special gift for sewing, and in my free time I devoted myself to it. Little by little, sewing became a passion. I was the one who had to mend the used clothes that would be distributed afterwards among people in the parish. I took care of the seams, the hems and the other alterations. I often dreamt of making a dress and choosing the pattern myself. Quite early on, I knew that sewing would be part of my life. The nuns often told me in fact that I was better at manual work than studying.

When I was sixteen, in 1928 to be more exact, I had an important encounter. Sometimes I accompanied the nuns outside the convent when they gave a helping hand to the Pères Eudistes, whom the bishop of Chicoutimi had entrusted in 1903 with the Parish of Sacré-Coeur. The parish priest and the curate were French Eudist fathers who had gone into exile in Canada because of the precarious situation of religious communities in France. To ensure the smooth running of the presbytery and to help the community, one of the fathers had brought back with him from a journey to Rennes three nuns of the congregation of the Soeurs Sainte-Marie de la Présentation: Sister Wenseslas, Sister Romuald, and Sister Adolphine. It's Sister Adolphine who, with Sister Marguerite, became my great confidant and mentor. She never ceased to encourage me, comfort me, and, if necessary, calm my anguish.

I would like to think that we didn't meet purely by chance and that this nun had been chosen to accompany me during the second part of my life. Sister Adolphine, too, discovered I had a talent for sewing, and encouraged me to persevere. She taught me haute couture, how to cut out a pattern and sew clothes. I eagerly applied myself to it. For the first time in my life, I realized I was happy, at last.

Sister Adolphine spoke French with a Breton accent, a musical quality that added a new flavour to my everyday existence. I even tried to imitate it, which made her laugh. I was fascinated by the distance she had covered to come all the way to us.

I often quizzed her about her country. I must have bothered her more than once, but her replies delighted me and made me want to travel.

This desire was completely new for me, even though my reading made me discover new horizons. Until that day, the idea of leaving had never entered my mind. My talks with the nun who had come from afar encouraged me, however, to explore territories other than my familiar surroundings. Besides, my education would soon be completed, and I would have to leave the convent school.

The Augustinian sisters weren't showing me the door, but they urged me to think about my future. After all the congregation had done for me, it would be right to pay my debt by becoming a member of the congregation, they said. So, when I was seventeen, I mentioned to Sister Adolphine that I would like to take the veil within the same community as hers. I indicated to her in this way how deeply I admired her.

The nun was thrilled, but she wanted me first to take part in a compulsory retreat for novices. The retreat would allow me to think things over thoroughly and find out if I really felt the call of God. She suggested a few considerations I might reflect on, such as the fact that by joining the ranks of the community, I would renounce the joys of motherhood. I should also ask myself if my love for God was powerful enough to make me accept all the heartbreaks without being overwhelmed with regrets for the rest of my life. "Because you are bound to have regrets at some time or other," she said.

Have I prayed enough to God to guide me on the path I believe to be mine? Am I ready to show a spirit of penitence and self-effacement and to glorify God at all times? In short, am I really willing to lead such an austere life?

I was much too young to be aware of all that was involved in such a decision. Those questions seemed abstract to me then. I couldn't really grasp their full meaning and certainly not their implications. Having only known the convent, I looked upon this calling as an occupation that would allow me to develop my talents as a dressmaker while I continued living a communal existence, as I always had.

To set my mind at ease, however, I asked Sister Adolphine what exactly one feels when one thinks one has been called. She said that if I had been summoned I would know it. But perhaps the call hadn't made itself heard yet, she added.

She also explained that to join her congregation one had to fulfill certain requirements. First of all, it was necessary to bring a dowry, as when a woman gets married. In 1929, the amount could be as high as $750. On the other hand, no candidate had ever been turned down on the grounds of a lack of money. Next, I had to agree to go through my novitiate at the congregation's mother house in Brittany. Even if I didn't have the money for the dowry, I would still need the funds for the trip. I felt wretched because I hadn't expected that becoming a nun would be so complicated.

When Sister Adolphine noticed my distress, she came to my aid once again. If my desire to join her congregation was sincere, she said, there might be a solution. She made an appointment with one of the curates of the parish. This priest had set up the Société Sainte-Marthe, which assisted needy girls. They immediately agreed to help me get the money together. Three months later, the Société Sainte-Marthe gave me $175. That was an achievement, especially in a time of crisis. Among my benefactors was a very wealthy couple from Chicoutimi. This amount made it possible for me to pay for the voyage across the Atlantic, which cost $27, and allowed me to have a few extra dollars for travelling and personal expenses. I gave the rest to the community. I had never thought, never even dreamt, that this journey could become a reality.

How lucky I was to be able to experience such an adventure in a foreign country. But I would only really believe it when the day of the great journey arrived. Time passed slowly, too slowly.

Leaving for Europe

A week before my adventure began, I couldn't keep still anymore. The preparations were complex and I found it terribly difficult to stay calm. The nuns had to call me to order several times. I talked too loudly, I laughed without reason. But how could anyone keep calm before such a grandiose undertaking? The experience I was about to embark on was most extraordinary for a girl like me. I was quite unprepared for it.

In all my young life, I had only known horse-drawn carriages. But to complete the long journey that would take me to the port of Saint-Malo in France, I had to travel by motor car, by train, and transatlantic liner!

The two nights before my departure, I just couldn't get to sleep. I tried to picture the various stages of the trip, but didn't succeed very well. Everything was confused and abstract. I had only seen trains, ocean liners, and the sea in photographs.

The night before leaving, I didn't sleep at all. I checked the contents of my suitcase several times, as thin as it was: some underwear, a black tunic, and a white blouse identical to the one I wore every day, two exercise books, a pencil, holy pictures, two white cotton head coverings that had to be worn to identify girls who were beginning their novitiate. I also took the old doll Sister Marguerite had given me when I first came to the convent and a personal letter from her.

I would reread it often all through my new life. She wished me good luck. In Europe, she said, I would be able to perfect my sewing skills because it was one of the best places in the world to do so. In Brittany, moreover, I would learn lace-making if I wanted to. She told me once again how dear I was to her and assured me she would always cherish me. I cried when I read that. Sister Marguerite was an extremely important woman to me. She was really my second mother.

❦ ❦ ❦

On October 15, 1930, I was eighteen and ready for the first day of the rest of my life.

As on every other morning, the wake-up bell rang at half past five. The two Eudist fathers and Sister Romuald, who would be travelling with us, would arrive at seven. Two other postulants from Chicoutimi were leaving with me to go through their novitiate in Europe: Sister Éva Tremblay and Sister Thérèse Martel, a cousin of mine whom I'd never met.

I washed, rushed through my breakfast, and made my way to the chapel to pray before leaving. I placed my fate in the hands of God and the Virgin Mary, in whom I had complete confidence. I asked them to guide me in this utterly unknown world. I confided my anxiety to them. I would no longer be sheltered as in the convent. I would be immersed in the outside world for over a week. The nuns had actually mentioned a ten-day journey to me. So I would be in contact with a huge number of people. "How should I act in society? That is why I ask you, God and merciful Blessed Virgin Mary, to protect me during this great odyssey."

Then I ran to the dormitory, although running was forbidden, picked up my suitcase, went to the convent's front door and waited as quietly as I could. It was half past six.

Two nuns who were talking to each other in the hall came up to remind me that the fathers wouldn't be here until about seven. I told them that time was passing too slowly and I would rather wait for them by the door. That way I could be sure they wouldn't forget me.

Fifteen minutes later, the two other postulants joined me in the doorway. They were just as overwrought as I was. We held hands. We needed to stay calm and definitely not shout.

Mother Superior came to give us her last recommendations. She warned us against strangers and made us promise we would always keep in sight of the nun who was in charge of us during the journey. She also gave us our legal papers. These enabled us to travel overseas under supervision. We were too young yet to have our own passports.

A funny noise reached us from outside. Everyone turned around and we saw the car, all black and shiny, with its four white-wall tires. I couldn't believe it. The automobile that would take us to the railway station was simply magnificent. It could hold six people.

I settled myself on the back seat and kept totally still. Only my fingers moved as I stroked the golden velvet of the seat. I was so excited I hardly dared take another breath, afraid to miss this unique moment. I tried to make myself tiny so no one would ask me to get out. Someone talked to me, but I didn't answer. In my nervousness I had forgotten my suitcase. I just wanted the automobile to get going. The driver switched on the ignition and we left. The huge car ran wonderfully smoothly. We barely felt the holes in the road and the stones, and that amazed us, since we were used to horse-drawn carriages shaking us energetically about whenever their wheels struck the slightest obstacle.

Already I prepared myself for the moment we would be asked to get out. The driver had left his window half open and I felt the chilly October wind on my cheeks. I closed my eyes and a great wave of happiness swept through me. I knew that from then on I would always love going for a drive.

Half an hour later, we arrived at the station. I stepped out of the car with a heavy heart. I would have wanted the ride to last longer. One of the fathers went to get the tickets. I was handed my suitcase with the warning to be careful not to lose it again. For the first time I saw the platform and my excitement grew.

Soon the train to Quebec City would enter the station at the scheduled time. If I already found the automobile huge, the train was even more astounding. It was interminably long and at least two storeys high. I was most impressed by its whistle announcing the train's entry into the station. As soon as I could, I climbed the three steps of the narrow stairs leading to the car where we were supposed to seat ourselves, and looked back to admire the station from my new vantage point.

The car's ceiling and walls were made of metal while the bench seats on either side were upholstered in black imitation leather. Some of the benches even allowed us to sit face to face with one another. After the size of the train, I think this surprised me the most. I don't know what came over me, but I ran to reserve a place on one of the benches. Astonished by my reaction, one of the fathers asked me to be a little less demonstrative and try to quiet down. He reminded me that given the number of hours we would spend on the train, I would have more than enough time to try all the seats, should I want to.

When I stepped into the dining-car a little later, I had to control myself all over again. I just stood there, flabbergasted. Unable to walk down the corridor and look for a seat, I obediently followed the nun who grabbed my arm and made me sit close to her at the table. I simply couldn't get over it. We could eat, sitting at a table, while the train travelled along! And, what's more, while admiring the passing scenery! I didn't miss a second of that first trip. It lasted five hours. I saw lakes, forests, farms, and animals slip by. It was like a picture book changing from page to page. When we arrived in Quebec City, we glimpsed the station in the distance before slowly entering it. It was as though we went into a castle surrounded by turrets. And I hadn't seen anything yet! There were still Montreal's Windsor Station and the station in New York to discover.

At a certain point, I forgot where I was. Travelling had tired me out, of course, but there was also all that nervous excitement at the many discoveries I made. I felt as if I were living a waking dream, too gigantic to be true. I became just a spectator, no longer experiencing the present moment, as if there was no more room in my eyes for new images. I had difficulty taking it all in. The fathers gave us a veritable history lecture by taking time to explain what we saw through the windows. My brain filled with all these explanations and I was overwhelmed by them.

I pulled myself together again in the automobile that took us from the station to the New York harbour. This car was called a taxi. I remember taking an instant liking to the word "taxi." It sounded like a foreign language.

What struck me first when I saw New York were, of course, the large number of skyscrapers. But I was especially amazed to see that the buildings were squeezed together on an island much smaller than the Saguenay–Lac-Saint-Jean territory. The fathers came to my aid once again. They explained that the reason there was such a density of buildings in this particular spot was that the soil lent itself to it, and this wasn't the case outside the area.

When we arrived at the harbour, we saw the majestic liner *France*, which would take us across the Atlantic. It was the only liner with four funnels and nothing like the photographs of ships I had seen at the convent. I was awestruck once more, and so overcome with emotion I felt like crying. My travel companions seemed as stunned as I was.

We were told how the boarding would proceed, but we were so excited we didn't understand a word of the fathers' explanations. We joined the lineup without really knowing where we were going. It was half past eight on the morning of October 17, and the virtual orphan Armande Martel was about to board the stately liner *France*. I who had resigned myself to living shut away in a convent for the rest of my days, was setting off toward a different destiny. It seemed unreal to me. Yet all I had done was tell Sister Adolphine that I wished to join her community. I never thought I would find myself thrust into the thick of an expedition like this.

We were guided through corridors to the space booked for us. It consisted of a large sitting room and two adjoining cabins, one of which, fitted out with berths, was reserved for us: the postulants and the nun.

My excitement reached fever pitch and made me forget my manners. Without consulting the others, I expressed my preference for sleeping in the upper berth. Luckily, no one objected, and I climbed into it. Up on my bed, I could see the toilet bowl and the tiny wash basin beside it. There was even a door we could close so we could wash ourselves in complete privacy. I couldn't believe it. I was beginning to understand the meaning of the word *luxury*. The fathers claimed on the other hand that the ship had deteriorated somewhat since the last time they sailed on it, a few years before, even though it still had a certain lustre. I decided to ignore their remarks. For me, it was the most beautiful ship in the world.

We quickly got ourselves settled and went out to walk around the decks. A lot of deck chairs were lined up there. I decided to lie down on one for a few seconds. I was called to order immediately. Leaning on the ship's railing — to me, it was the "balcony balustrade" — we watched the activity in the harbour. Many automobiles drove up and discharged batches of new passengers, who rushed up the gangway while workers pushed along carts loaded with luggage, food, and all sorts of bottles.

Beside me, a couple was in the middle of a discussion. The lady said she was worried about the ocean voyage because she still remembered what happened to the *Titanic*, which sank in 1912, the year I was born. Her husband tried to reassure her. He explained that the sinking was due in part to human error. This argument seemed to reassure her, as it did me, in fact. I had absolutely no desire to make the voyage while dreading some looming misfortune.

We continued looking around the decks, from port side to starboard. There was an area set aside for "sunbathing," but we were forbidden to go there, of course. Besides the main deck, we counted six others. At the centre of the ship was a magnificent staircase, with wrought-iron railings, connecting the promenade deck with the upper deck. There were also two elevators giving access to the upper storeys.

We entered a large, luxurious lounge. Sitting on velvet-upholstered chairs around little tables, people were talking while having coffee, tea, or alcoholic drinks. The adjoining dining room was extremely grand with its glass chandeliers, immaculate white tablecloths, and china tableware. We wouldn't have the good fortune to see it sparkle brilliantly at night with its diners in evening dress, since we were to eat in the cabin. It would be an enchanting sight, I thought. Our chaperones didn't want to show us the huge ballroom because, I imagine, they were anxious to keep us away from the temptation of sin.

We then sat down in the cafeteria and for the first time in my life I had a scrumptious ham sandwich.

An announcement was made that the ship would leave in an hour. Awaiting that moment, the postulants and I exchanged our first impressions while the fathers talked to other passengers. It was a glorious mid-October day and rather warm. We were told that the holds were finally full and a siren would soon sound the departure. It was a good thing they had let us know, otherwise we all would have jumped when we heard the shrill blast of that siren. Then the engines started up noisily, giving off a nasty fuel-oil smell. The odour made Éva Tremblay very unwell; I even thought she was going to faint.

All the passengers were out on the decks to watch the great departure manoeuvres. It was spectacular. Slowly the ship pulled away from the docks and the tugboats darted ahead as they began towing us to the open sea, since the engines couldn't run at full throttle in such shallow water. The *France*, according to what we caught from conversations around us, was the third-fastest liner on the North Atlantic.

I suddenly felt very small in the middle of that vast expanse of inky black water and wondered by what kind of phenomenon such a gigantic thing was able to float. When the coast disappeared on the horizon, I panicked a little. On the third day, an underwater storm tossed the ship about for several hours and I thought the sea was simply going to swallow us up. The *France*, so colossal in the harbour a couple of days ago, now, faced with the raging sea, felt like a tiny paper boat. Éva, who hadn't had a thing to eat since we left New York, felt worse and worse. The doctor told her she should consume some food, even if she remained lying in her berth. Her stomach needed to fill up, which would have a pendulum effect and prevent retching. But it didn't work with her. As for me, as soon as the ocean was calm, I went out on deck. The sea air did me the world of good. And because it was cold outside, there were few passengers on the deck. So no one bothered me.

As we approached the coast of Europe, I had a chance to admire the fine residences near the harbour. They were very different from the buildings in Quebec. I instantly fell in love with the new land that was taking me in.

In the early morning of October 21, we dropped anchor in the harbour of Le Havre. While the ship drew alongside the quay, we were all out on the deck already and watched the people who had come to wave a welcome to the *France*. I felt as though I was coming home and imagined that in that crowd a family was waiting for me. All the passengers seemed very happy to reach dry land again after the long Atlantic crossing. Only Éva hadn't enjoyed the ocean voyage and was just as pale as when we first set out.

A transportation service conveyed us to the railway station. The train would first take us to Paris, then to Brittany. It would be about a twelve-hour trip. So the fathers who travelled with us recommended we have patience. We needed lots of it: I was terribly anxious to get to the new convent. Once on board, I took advantage of the opportunity to admire the scenery, so totally different from that of Quebec. As we approached Paris, I became tremendously excited. Sister Adolphine had told me a great deal about Paris, which people called the City of Lights, the place where all the great fashion designers were located. That was very important to me. I couldn't wait to start sewing again and learn new techniques as I had been promised. To pass the time, I isolated myself in an out-of-the way corner of the railway car and sketched styles of dresses worn by ladies aboard the ship or the trains. These drawings would have to stay in my notebooks, of course, because the nuns would never agree to my making clothes for lay people. But no one could stop me from dreaming.

In the early evening we finally arrived in Brittany, at the station of Rennes, the town where the mother house of the community of the Filles de Sainte-Marie de la Présentation was situated. A kind, thoughtful nun met us on the platform. I recognized Sister Adolphine's accent right away. It warmed my heart. Through hearing that voice all the time, I had grown used to it.

At last we reached the end of our journey. I had sometimes thought it would never end. Several nuns were waiting for us at the entrance of the convent. And what a convent! It was huge. Again, I couldn't believe my eyes and stood admiring its architecture for a few long moments before going inside. How many years had it taken to construct such a colossal building? I couldn't say. But I had never seen stone walls as massive as these. You would think you were in a fortress. I already felt safe. Though tired from the journey, I mustered up the energy to walk around the premises and meet all those who lived here.

The convent was at least four times as large as the one where I grew up. How would I manage not to get lost in the beginning? I recognized the smells of my old convent, those of floor polish, oiled woodwork, and disinfectant. Though at first these smells had put me off, with the passing of time they had become part of my daily life.

A nun kindly showed us around our new quarters, but because of her strong accent I missed some of her explanations.

Except for a few details, the dormitory was identical to the one I had first set eyes on when I was six years old. This time, however, it struck me as pleasant. A new life was beginning for me and I had a taste for learning and for savouring every moment. I found our hostesses delightfully friendly and, above all, very patient with us, the "little nuns from Canada," as they called us. I was happy to discover that the community's rules of life were much less strict than in Quebec, and the chores less heavy and more varied.

After a light meal of bread and cheese, we went to bed. We badly needed to, especially Éva, who had to stay in the infirmary for a week to recover from the journey.

Two days after our arrival, Thérèse Martel and I took off again to receive our novitiate training on Guernsey, a Channel island about a hundred kilometres off St. Malo. The boat trip lasted a day, but since I came from afar, that didn't frighten me at all. On the eight-kilometre-long island, automobiles were driven on the left-hand side of the road, as in England; the currency in use was the pound sterling. People earned their living in the shipbuilding industry and from fishing. Fish, in fact, was something I would eat my fill of on this island.

When we landed on Guernsey, we were taken to the parish of Sainte-Marie-du-Câtel, where the community's second house, La Chaumière, was located. This is where the nuns did their novitiate training. With its varnished woodwork throughout, the house, more modest than the mother house at Rennes, had a rustic character. In the garden grew many fruit trees. It was a friendly, peaceful spot, and I could understand why Victor Hugo chose to go and write on this island.

The low-ceilinged dormitory was particularly inviting. The beds were wonderfully soft and so comfortable that I savoured my sleep every night of my stay.

I soon familiarized myself with the organization of the house and was assigned to the kitchen. I tried to quickly memorize the names of the cooking utensils by jotting them down on a piece of paper. Most of the French names were different from the Quebec ones and I found them prettier. Thus, a ladle was a *cassotte*, a conical mesh sieve a *chinois*, a potato masher a *presse-purée*. A *marguerite* was used to steam vegetables and a *pince à chiqueter* to crimp the edge of a tart.

I worked at preparing meals while discovering new flavours, spices, and smells. This country life satisfied me completely.

On Guernsey, I also got to know the community's values. In the opinion of the Abbé Fleury, the founder, we shouldn't become ladies, but sisters of charity. "Always be content with your lot," he would say. Sisters needed to strive to attain evangelic simplicity in all their activities. Their zeal ought to be imbued with true generosity, never flinching at any task. They must remain serene at all times, in good fortune as in bad. In a word, we ought to attain the calm and cheerful humility that expands the soul and infuses its devotion with the artlessness described by Saint Francis de Sales.

On girls whose thoughts are filled with generous ideas, who are enthralled with perfection, and feel impelled toward the cloister, the Divine Master has cast His eye. Quietly He speaks to them and draws them to Him. They should always remember the words of one of our founders, Louise Lemarchand: "You will be a nun ... Jesus needs you. He wants you all to Himself. He counts on you to serve Him and love Him ..." Mademoiselle Lemarchand also said that nuns must be good, devout, and strong, and, above all, have no taste for society life, because the world around them is spiritually beneath them.

It was the first time I heard the religious life described this way. There was no mention whatsoever of the obligation to experience the emotion of faith or God's call. The image of God as a master had never crossed my mind. Surprisingly, this religious philosophy seemed to be based on resentment against life outside the convent, whereas everything I had seen, heard, and experienced of the outside world since the beginning of this epic, had struck me as stimulating. I wasn't able to put into words how I felt, but such a view seemed nevertheless quite oppressive to me, and as a result I was less at ease in this milieu. Naturally I kept my doubts to myself.

On July 11, 1931, I took my first, temporary, vows, which allowed me to begin my novitiate. I was nineteen.

That day, the postulants had to follow a protocol. After we got dressed, our hair was cut. This represented a big sacrifice for me because I loved my long, black, curly hair. *Never mind*, I thought, *it will grow again*. I didn't have time to pine for the past and didn't want to spoil such a beautiful occasion. I was nervous but, more than anything else, I longed to become a novice. I imagined I would become a different person: Every day I would feel, deep inside, the state of grace in which my pure soul dwelled. How naive I was!

All the postulants had donned a little black dress, which was shorter than the nuns', with a white collar, and put on a silver cross without the figure of Christ, strung on a silk cord. On our heads we wore a black veil over a white headband.

The ceremony resembled in every respect a first communion. Seated in the pews of the chapel, we listened to the nuns as they guided our thoughts. They asked us once more if we were certain about our choice and if our decision had been made of our own free will. How can you be sure about the path to take when you are just nineteen? As for me, my decision had been firm for a long time. It was the only way of life I knew.

Then the priest spoke in our name and repeated one by one the vows of poverty, chastity, and obedience we were to profess. At the end of the ceremony, the congregation gave a great banquet in the garden, at the back of the house. It was an unforgettable day.

During the two years of my novitiate, I applied myself to the tasks assigned to me, and sewed in my free time.

In the summer after I arrived, I was asked to look after eight children in the country while their parents worked. There were at least eight children in nearly every island family. All the parents were fishermen and farmers. About the people living on Guernsey, Victor Hugo once said: "The same man farms the land and the sea." I adored my experience with the children. I remembered my childhood in the company of my brothers, so it did me a lot of good to be in contact with them.

After the holidays, when the new school year began, I went back to the convent and resumed my work in the kitchens. But living with a family for a few weeks had made me aware of my loneliness. As time passed, I had felt more and more isolated on Guernsey; news from the outside was slow to reach us. We rarely saw new faces. We were at the mercy of ships and the weather. When the sea raged, we didn't receive anything. Deep inside, I felt abandoned, too.

I cheered myself up with the thought that I only had to spend one more winter on this remote island, and on July 5, 1933, my novitiate would be completed. I would go back to Rennes then, to the mother house.

Second Notebook

My Vows and the War

After a nearly two-year stay on the island of Guernsey, I went back to the congregation's mother house at Rennes. The time had come to prepare myself for the perpetual vows I was to take at the end of the last year of my novitiate.

In the course of that year, I continued my religious training by attending classes in natural theology and dogmatic theology. I seriously believed I was incapable of absorbing this teaching. I had doubts as to my ability to master this science which, I thought, was only intended for great thinkers. The nuns were quick to reassure me. Studying theology, they explained, meant primarily concerning oneself with God. Natural theology spoke of the existence of God, demonstrated His divine attributes as well as His eternity, perfection, goodness, and omnipotence. Theology of the religious life initiated us to prayer, taught us how to live the liturgy in the community, how to keep God's Word in our hearts and embody it afterwards in the world.

We novices had a very full morning program. We got up at five and attended Dawn Prayer and Matins. This was the shortest of the day's five services. Next, we had breakfast while listening to a spiritual reading. Then we went into class. After that, we went to the service of the Liturgy of the Hours, and then came the midday meal. Once the meal was over, we attended another service of the Liturgy of the Hours before going back into class. In the late afternoon, we attended one more service of the liturgy, before the evening meal. Vespers came next, right after supper, followed, believe it or not, by obligatory recreation. May I point out that I would have taken part in it even if I hadn't been obliged to?

At half past seven, while going to bed, we had to observe total silence.

On Sundays, after High Mass, we finally had a bit of free time to take care of personal matters. It was the only free time we had.

In that last year of my novitiate, I became friends with a girl whose real name I didn't know. We had to remain anonymous. When the day came to take her perpetual vows, this friend wanted to choose the name Marie-Louise, in honour of Mademoiselle Louise Lemarchand, one of our community's founders. That's what I called her.

We had developed a close bond, mainly through our common passion for sewing. She was born in Rennes, into a family of working people. Her father carried out jobs for the community. Marie-Louise had been in contact with the nuns for much of her childhood and as a result greatly admired them. She told me she had clearly felt the call to the religious life, and I envied her for that.

Marie-Louise was, like me, in her last novitiate year. We shared all our sewing tricks. I told her about Sister Adolphine, who had taught me so much about the art of dressmaking. That was all I could think of before going to sleep and I often designed clothes in my notebooks, which I had never shown to anyone.

On Sundays, we exchanged what we had learned up to then, like the cross-stitch, commonly used to make a strong seam; overcasting, meant to keep a fabric from fraying; or the running stitch, for invisible hems. We also talked about haute couture. We wondered how many hours it would take us to sew, by hand, a dress sketched by a fashion designer. A nearly impossible task, we thought. We fantasized together about design and tailoring. Sunday afternoons flew by this way and were wonderfully stimulating. We would start the new week of classes with fresh energy.

We also had retreats, called "vocation retreats," where we questioned ourselves about our faith. I took advantage of these periods of contemplation to ask myself if I might possibly have received the call of God and the religious life without actually being aware of it. I didn't remember receiving an unmistakable call like Sister Marie-Louise's. And what exactly were you supposed to feel?

To help us reflect on this question, the community had drawn up a list:

> You experience God's call if your taste for
> prayer and your affection for Jesus Christ are
> unwavering; if, from time to time, you have felt
> stirring within you a desire to become a nun; if
> you do not care about money, or possessions,
> or about dominating others; if you are able to
> live a simple life and like living communally, as
> a member of a group.

I did feel more or less everything on this list, but perhaps not intensely enough. *The* big question tormenting me was: "Do I love God sufficiently?" I obviously loved God, except that the term "sufficiently" made me hesitate. Just how great was this love? And wasn't my desire to become a nun the logical result of the first part of my life at the convent?

The nuns had often told me that it was thanks to the community and to the education I received there that I had become the exemplary woman I was. They also emphasized the fact that I had never wanted for anything. Did I feel so indebted to the nuns that I would devote the rest of my life to them, though I was only twenty-two?

Communities often expected orphans they had taken care of to become nuns. It seemed like a natural way to pay back what they had spent on us. I think that was the idea they were trying to convey to me. I realized, though, that, if I agreed to this destiny, my future would consist of servitude, obedience, and complete submission. Despite these reservations, I was happy.

During my self-examination, I never once questioned my vow of chastity. Of course I felt certain desires once in a while that struck me as abnormal, but at those times I tried to take my mind off things. I would get up, write in my notebooks, or pray. There was no question of my admitting to these urges in confession; what happened between *me* and *me*, I said to myself, only concerned *me*.

I would soon be married to God, and marriage was the most important thing for a twenty-two-year-old girl. We were going to give our life to God forever. To me, it was a great mystery, however, because this union wasn't something tangible. And at that age, what does "forever" mean? Never mind my uncertainties, I took my perpetual solemn vows in the month of Mary, on the first Sunday in May of the year 1934.

This marriage to the Lord was a grandiose ceremony. The convent's chapel overflowed with white flowers. There were about forty of us taking the veil that day. We were all very nervous. One sensed a feverish excitement in the air, as on the morning of a wedding.

Mass was celebrated first. Then, after the reading of a passage from the Gospel, began the ritual of the interrogations concerning our oaths. This is when I whispered my first "yes," which bound me to the community's rules. Next, we prostrated ourselves, lying face downward on the ground, while the other nuns sang the Liturgy of the Saints.

I was anxious and worried, unsure whether I had grasped the deeper meaning of my commitment. Had I properly understood that I agreed to live all my life in poverty, chastity, and obedience? I chose the name Sister Marie-Noëlle, simply because it was both the name of the Virgin and her son's day of birth.

The great event ended in a gargantuan buffet. I had never seen so much food. I discovered right then the pleasures of gluttony, one of the seven deadly sins, and this in spite of the vows I had just professed!

I now had a new status, being Sister Marie-Noëlle, a new habit, and a ring on my finger. The day following that memorable ceremony, I was also assigned to a new task, that of the laundry. In order to learn the various stages of the cleaning of clothes and bedding, I had to be trained for six months by the sister in charge. In the beginning I was very keen, but after a week I felt totally exhausted. At suppertime I couldn't keep my eyes open. Same thing during evening prayers.

The heat and humidity on the premises were unbearable. Moreover, my new habit was made of thicker fabric than the uniform I wore as a novice, to say nothing of the coarse-cotton apron that helped to protect my habit. And it was only May. What would it be like in summer? When I mentioned to the sister in charge how exhausted I was, she replied curtly, "You'll just have to get used to it, Sister!" I knew then and there that whatever my state of mind or malaise might be, no one would have any compassion. I had to endure everything without complaining. At that moment I hit upon the idea of making a habit that would be identical to the one we wore, but of a material twice as light. It would be reserved exclusively for nuns working on these premises. I talked about it with Sister Marie-Louise, who was thrilled to go and search for a fabric with me that would allow our skins to breathe. Our choice fell on linen, a natural fibre, which we would be able to dye black.

The day we could finally put on our new linen garb, the twenty-six nuns who worked with me appeared very much relieved. In the meantime, I had had to learn the tough job of laundering.

I had never realized that cleaning clothes could be such an arduous chore. One piece of washing could go through our hands thirteen times before being returned, spotless, to its starting point: everything had to be collected, sorted, coupled, marked, washed, rinsed, starched, wrung out, dried, ironed, folded, assembled, and delivered. The nuns placed their clothes in a net bag that had their name and number on it. As soon as the bag arrived at the laundry, the clothes were sorted into three categories: light-coloured clothes, thick clothes, and heavily soiled clothes. Every day of the week was identified by a thread of a different colour, which was pinned on each garment so that all garments would be dealt with in order of arrival. Then we needed to sew the small, more personal, items together so they wouldn't get lost. My first task was to gather up the dirty socks, handkerchiefs, underpants, and sanitary napkins, which were in fact nothing but rags, since we didn't have anything that was disposable. This operation was called "coupling." It was a rather revolting job, and while carrying it out, I was often very close to bringing up my breakfast.

A few months later, I was put in charge of the ironing of sheets, pillowcases, and tablecloths. Creases were not tolerated. The supervising sister had noticed that I had an aptitude for this work. Even though my new task wasn't easy, it was far less exhausting than wringing out sheets, which I had been doing previously. To remove as much water as possible, we had to fold the heavy, soaking wet sheets, wring them, and then beat them on a large washboard.

In 1937, I moved into the residence of the Eudist fathers, fifty-five kilometres from ours. I worked in the laundry there, too, and performed the same tasks. Although I found it strange to see a procession of men's garments and undergarments go past me, at least I didn't have to deal with soiled menstruation cloths anymore.

They had settled me in a little room I had all to myself. What a relief, since I had been feeling greatly in need of some privacy these past few months. I wasn't complaining, but being on my own did me the world of good. The room was fitted out with a small white metal bed topped by a black crucifix, a chest of drawers, a tiny table and chair, and a hook to hang up my nun's habit.

Right away, I felt happy there. I could write in my diary without fear of prying eyes. I particularly enjoyed being able to take off my robe and veil as soon as I walked in. I would double-lock the door, since I was only wearing my underclothes. It was a truly liberating experience for me because I disliked having my head covered at all times. I would scratch my scalp for a good ten minutes. Finally the air could circulate over my skin, and that was very pleasant. In summer, I would close my eyes and lie stretched out on my bed like this and savour the cool of the night. In short, I was delighted with my new little home.

There were about forty nuns working for the fathers. The evening meal was taken in a refectory fitted out for our use. My seat was very near the three sisters in charge of the various maintenance departments.

It was during one of these meals that I first heard about Adolf Hitler and the rumours of war that were going around.

It was the spring of 1939, and several fathers of the congregation were talking among themselves about this man who seemed to be feared far and wide. He threatened to wage war on all European countries, and the fathers believed that another world war might well break out. One month later, I was asked to go to the congregation's mother house because Mother

Superior wanted to see me. Six Canadian nuns were sent for like this. Mother Superior told us that the rumours about a looming global conflict worried her.

She informed us that to divert the attention away from the "foreigners" we were, we would have to travel back and forth continually between Guernsey and Brittany during the summer in order to cover our tracks and prevent the French authorities from making us return to Canada. She would do everything in her power to protect us, but couldn't predict the future.

Although I hadn't forgotten about my birthplace, Chicoutimi, since living in Brittany, the idea of going back at some point was the farthest thing from my mind. What for? For my family, whom I had never seen again apart from a single visit from my father? To serve my community? I was serving it very well over here. If there was one feeling I had never experienced in all my young life, it was definitely "homesickness."

If it's true that human beings are destined to have several lives, I must have lived in Brittany in a former one because I felt completely at home there. I had quickly adapted myself to the customs, the food, and the attitude of the people, and I loved the way they spoke. I could easily have stayed in Brittany until the end of my days.

So, from May to August, we made many trips back and forth between the nuns' residence on Guernsey and the monastery of the Eudist fathers, where I went back to work as soon as I returned.

The tension in the world appeared to have risen by a notch, and we rarely went out into the gardens because the people of Rennes were growing increasingly afraid of strangers. Never having lived through such a conflict, I was unaware of the gravity of the events. The religious life was a comfortable cocoon, in which prayer played a major part. I was completely ignorant of the issues of this war. Moreover, no one informed us of new developments on the international scene. Only snatches of conversation reached us during the evening meal. It was precious little.

On September 3, 1939, around ten o'clock in the morning, the village bells and sirens announced that we were at war. Mother Superior sent for us again to explain what was happening, while trying to keep us from panicking.

The leaders of our community avoided talking about the war with the young sisters. They tried to spare us the horror this global conflict might create. Every day, they strengthened the protective shield around the mother house, while warning us of certain dangers hanging particularly over the "little Canadians." England had declared war on Germany after Hitler invaded Poland. As a result, we Canadians, being British subjects, became Hitler's enemies.

When I left the nun's office that day, I was in a state of shock. The tone of her voice as she uttered that last sentence resounded in my head. It suddenly struck me that I had become an outlaw and absolutely had to hide. A sense of urgency gripped me; I wanted to go back to my country.

I asked to see Mother Superior again. She received me in her office. I shared my fears with her and said I wanted to return to Canada. She replied that she had already been trying for some time to have us repatriated, but the travel documents had so far failed to arrive. Five months had passed since her first request. She was very concerned and couldn't foresee what would happen to us. She ended our conversation by promising she would let me know as soon as she found out more.

The mood in the monastery of the Eudist fathers grew tenser by the day. I still worked in the laundry, and we were afraid the Germans might decide to come and get us. They now occupied the town. We didn't go out anymore. When we caught a glimpse of a group of soldiers passing our windows, we hid immediately. We jumped at the slightest noise.

There was nothing we could pin our hopes on. Our papers still hadn't arrived and Mother Superior was becoming quite guarded. The five other Canadians and I all felt that something serious was going to happen.

The Arrest

It was around eight o'clock in the morning, December 5, 1940, when German soldiers knocked on the door of 31, rue d'Antrain, the residence of the Eudist fathers. They asked to see me immediately. The nun who let them in hurriedly sent someone to warn the sister in charge, in the absence of the superior sister, before going to get me at the laundry where I worked.

When I stepped into the entrance hall, breathless and terrified, the sister in charge was already there. She took me firmly by the arm to support and comfort me, while, in heavily accented French, one of the soldiers read out the document they had come to deliver to me.

> As of now, you must consider yourself a prisoner. You must not leave your apartment; we will come to get you. You must take warm clothes.
> Any attempt to evade this order will result in the death penalty.

The soldier added that they would come back for me in a few days. Before leaving, they clicked their heels, raised their arms into the air, and shouted, *"Heil Hitler!"* I flinched and felt my blood run cold. I didn't grasp what was happening. I stood there, paralyzed. The nun in charge had to take me by the arm and lead me to my little room. Mother Superior would be back in a few hours, she said. She would be able to help me understand my situation. I splashed my face with cold water to bring myself back to reality. I couldn't believe my ears: the soldier really had mentioned the death penalty! I read the document they'd given me. My hands wouldn't stop shaking.

The words "prisoner" and "death penalty" were well and truly there. I could die, then, simply because I was a Canadian citizen! That didn't make sense. My crime was being a British subject. It was all so abstract for me since I had never even set foot in England! My allegiance to the British crown was limited to having seen a few pictures of the king and queen. There had to be some other purpose for my arrest...where were the Germans going to take me? I wondered. Perhaps they simply wanted to send me back to Canada. I hoped so.

The superior sister arrived at last and I was brought to her office. By way of reassurance, she told me that the other Canadian nuns had received the same notice. She explained that England refused to become Germany's ally and Hitler had therefore given orders on November 16, 1940, to arrest all British subjects in the occupied zone.

My knowledge of political matters was extremely limited, so I couldn't understand why I was being threatened with the death penalty. I panicked. I summed up my predicament: If I didn't obey orders, I would die merely because I was born in a country that was protected by another country that didn't want to fight for Germany. Really! It was unbelievable I would be killed for that reason! I wouldn't even be entitled to a trial, wouldn't even be able to defend myself. The superior sister replied calmly, "My dear child, we must submit. Those are the facts and there is nothing we can do about it."

I cried for hours. I didn't want to live anymore. I barely ate. My mind conjured up the worst possible outcomes. To get rid of these morbid thoughts, I tried to convince myself that the Germans only wanted to repatriate me to Canada.

The fateful day arrived. I was asked to pack my bags and take enough provisions to last me for forty-eight hours.

Three nuns of our community had been arrested: my cousin Thérèse Martel, who had become Sister Saint-Jean-de-Brébeuf, Éva Tremblay, who was now Sister Marie-Wilbrod, and I.

A truck picked us up and took us to the town hall of Rennes. The three of us made a point of staying very close together; I clung as tightly as I could to the two other nuns. We were told that, since the occupation began, this building had become one of the headquarters of the German army. Our documents were checked. Then we were informed of our destination. I still believed they had arrested the wrong person and I would be allowed to go home. I was handed a piece of paper that stated in German where I would be sent. Needless to say I didn't understand a word of that language. I only recognized my name, my town, and my passport number.

As I waited at the police station, my fear grew and grew. The two nuns beside me were sure the Germans were going to send us to an internment camp. I then asked people around me what "internment camp" meant. They told me it was a place where those who were arrested were sent and forced to work.

At three in the afternoon, another truck came to get us at the town hall. The two other nuns and I seated ourselves on a wooden bench at the back of the van, as far away from the Germans as possible, so they couldn't see us cry, as we said to each other. I was inconsolable. I trembled all over. My cousin and I held each other's hand so tightly that our fingers went numb.

Suddenly a woman got up and tried to jump out of the moving truck. A soldier caught her by the arm and forced her to sit down again by striking her hard in the ribs with the butt of his rifle.

My trembling grew worse and I hid my face in my veil so as not to see anything anymore. Sister Marie-Wilbrod put her arms around my cousin and me and tried to quiet us down. She remained calm and wasn't crying. I wondered how she managed to control herself while being confronted like us with an extremely violent act for the first time in her life.

The truck stopped on the way to pick up other prisoners, one of them a seventy-two-year-old Frenchwoman who was arrested because she had been married to a British subject, even though she had been divorced for a long time.

Most of them didn't understand what was happening and seemed just as terrorized as we were. The soldiers kept their weapons aimed in our direction at all times and glared at us.

We arrived at the station, where a train was waiting for us. In the first car, whose door was open, an enormous machine gun stood on a platform. The doors of the other cars were sealed. The small air vents were blocked with barbed wire. The soldiers made us get into one of the cars. Then, at five o'clock, the train slowly started moving. I was overcome by despair and thought of my brothers and my father in the Saguenay. They knew nothing about my fate! But realistically, how could they come to my aid?

We travelled for five nights and four days. We had to change trains several times. Eventually we lost all sense of time and place. The soldiers continued to fill the cars with new prisoners.

Toward the end of our journey there were about seventy of us in our car, all crammed together in unsanitary conditions. Sometimes we travelled for more than twelve hours without being able to urinate. Finally the inevitable happened. Several people urinated right there. Others had diarrhea.

The train stopped at last, in the middle of the night, in what appeared to be a cattle station. No one knew what was happening. We heard cries and the sound of boots outside.

In the small hours we were ordered to get out. Six abreast, escorted by soldiers, we marched on each side of the road like a troop of sleepwalkers. We had hardly slept at all for several days. The few people we met on the side of the road seemed surprised to see us and murmured, "They're even arresting nuns!" We finally learned we were going to the Vauban barracks at Besançon.

Most of the prisoners were Americans by birth. They had been arrested for that reason alone, although the war had only just been declared. There were also citizens of the Commonwealth, like me. I found out later that twenty-four hundred women, mainly of British extraction, including six hundred nuns, had been interned in the Vauban barracks at Besançon. The citadel, which comprised several buildings, was designed to accommodate soldiers, not women.

We were taken to building B, where we were able to find a place to sleep. Stretchers served as bunks and everyone tried to locate the cleanest and most respectable-looking one before covering it with a straw mattress, pulled from a stack at the building's entrance.

Our group of nuns settled itself in a corner, apart from the others. We were all exhausted, but that didn't stop us from reciting a hopeful prayer. I fell asleep immediately after.

In the morning, we were woken up by loudspeakers. We were ordered to go and get our food. There weren't enough dishes for everyone. We managed as best we could by washing the few bowls we found in the drinking trough for the horses. In any case, we were only entitled to a watery liquid of a questionable colour, which bore no resemblance to tea or coffee.

At noon, they served us ice-cold vegetables, including potatoes and turnips. For supper, we were entitled to a sauce streaked with blood. There was no way of knowing what animal the blood was from. I felt a wave of revulsion when I saw that fare. My legs went limp, and I collapsed on the ground in tears.

Sister Marie-Wilbrod helped me up and did her best to comfort me, telling me to try to be brave and strong because our troubles weren't over. No one knew how long we would stay in this camp. How could I keep my spirits up under such conditions until this torture ended?

My new address was Frontstalag 142. Several prisoners had grown weaker by waiting in long lines for our meagre sustenance. Every day, we needed to line up three times like that. There were on average fifteen daily deaths caused by malnutrition. We had to wait outside for hours while the dampness and chill went right through our clothes. I considered myself lucky to be wearing my nun's garments, because they gave me some protection against the cold, which wasn't the case for most of the other prisoners. Our headdresses had been tossed out, but we still had our veils and headbands.

Dysentery began ravaging the camp. The toilets had been set up outside, and there were many sick people who fell down on the stairs while making their way toward them, and sometimes they died on the spot.

In our building, the stretchers were all jammed up against each other. The women were embarrassingly close to one another. The prisoners' smell became intolerable at times and made me nauseous. I had never thought I would be able to bear such a stench. We only had very little water at our disposal to bathe ourselves. Besides, the water that came out of the taps was terribly cold and, since there was no heating in the building, we didn't dare get undressed to wash.

A few days after we arrived at the camp, we noticed that our straw mattresses were infested with bugs. Under those circumstances sleeping became practically impossible. Gloomily I kept wondering when this nightmare would end. As exhausted as I was, I took comfort in the thought that I was healthy and there were prisoners who needed me.

The soldiers assigned us certain tasks. Sister Marie-Wilbrod and I were ordered to deliver medicines to sick prisoners. So we assisted Dr. Gilet, a prisoner himself, in his duties, the doctor being unable to cope with the task on his own.

Every evening, we made the rounds of the buildings with our box containing pills for sore throats, liniment for aching muscles, and rhubarb pills against constipation. This job did me the world of good. It drove away my black thoughts. Night after night I waited for the moment when I finally felt useful.

Every now and then, as we did our rounds, German soldiers tried to talk to us. They showed us pictures of their children. Seeing nuns held as prisoners must have stirred up feelings of remorse in some of them. Immediately other soldiers would move toward us, and that put an end to the attempts to communicate.

One of them asked us at some point to treat his sore throat. Sister Marie-Wilbrod advised him to go and see a German nurse. She would have been able to help him, but was too worried about the consequences. "We can never be careful enough in our situation," she warned me.

When we got back from our rounds, shortly before curfew, the Germans were counting the prisoners and searching our straw mattresses to make sure we hadn't hidden any weapons in them. From time to time they brought us a bit of bread. They must have thought they were being generous. Although the bread was hard as a rock, ash-grey, and already mouldy, we ate it anyway. Hunger gnawed at us too much. The food parcels sent by our religious community rarely reached us.

Since I couldn't stop myself from writing, I kept a diary, but was afraid the soldiers might find it. We were often alerted about searches by other women prisoners. Then I hid my notebook in a fold of my habit. Sister Marie-Wilbrod, my cousin, and some other women in the camp had already warned me against possible reprisals if my diary were ever found. They had witnessed all sorts of atrocities for acts much less serious than mine. But I disregarded their advice because writing, for me, was life itself.

One day, about fifty novices of the congregation of the Petites Soeurs des Pauvres entered the camp. The oldest one, who was in charge, pleaded with the commandant to let us have the services of a priest. A few days later, he sent us a priest, an internee himself. From then on, Mass was celebrated daily. This ritual was a great comfort to us and helped us endure captivity. We had set up a small chapel where we could go during the day to pray. Since the camp commandant was a Catholic, we were able to attend Midnight Mass on December 25, 1940. There were some soldiers present.

The Red Cross watched over us and even provided decks of cards for our entertainment.

From time to time, there were air raid warnings. Sirens would wail. The German soldiers immediately ran into the shelters, whereas we had to stay where we were. So we wouldn't be too alarmed, we told ourselves that the Allies weren't going to bomb us.

In January of 1941, the Red Cross of Geneva visited our camp. After meeting the authorities, it drew up an incriminating report about the state of the premises, denouncing the unsanitary conditions in which we were kept. To put pressure on the officials, Winston Churchill threatened to deport all Germans interned in Great Britain to Canada. This threat was taken seriously because two months later, luggage in hand, we left for a camp with better amenities, at Vittel, in the Vosges. The Germans had requisitioned several hotels, and we were taken to one of them.

Vittel was a holiday resort, renowned for its thermal springs. About two thousand people were interned there, mainly Americans, Russians, British citizens, and Polish and Austrian Jews holding obviously fake British and American passports.

So we had a new address: Frontstalag 121. The grounds were surrounded by six-metre-high barbed wire, and anyone attempting to climb over it was in trouble. Because we had moved into a large hotel, we all needed to be disinfected. The showers were in continuous use for several days. In particular, the bugs we had brought in our luggage needed to be exterminated, since we now slept in clean beds with sheets. We had dishes, and the building was neat. We were convinced that God was taking things in hand. The quality of the food didn't really change, although sauerkraut was added to the menu, but it was so salty it was inedible.

Life was easier in Vittel. There were facilities outside the hotel for exercising, even for playing tennis and volleyball. In the afternoon, my cousin and I used to go for a stroll in the hotel gardens.

It was during one of these outings that we first heard about Hitler's extreme hatred of the Jewish people. A young girl, barely fourteen years old, approached us as we walked along. Her name was Anny. She told us that she and her family were Americans living in France. Her mother was in the infirmary because she'd had a baby. In the bed next to her mother's lay a woman who cried constantly and seemed inconsolable. According to Anny's mother, that woman, who was Austrian, had also just had a baby. She was crying because she was alone. Her whole family had been sent to concentration camps, except her. Thanks to her husband she had been able to hide her Jewish identity and obtain forged papers for herself and her baby. Now she was afraid the soldiers would discover her real name and take the baby away from her so they could send her to a camp. Young Anny thought that we, the nuns, had more influence than lay people. With all the naïveté of a girl her age, she asked us if we could take the baby with us and convince the Germans that its parents were dead. She was sure that, since there were many children at the hotel, the soldiers would believe our story. It's true that a large number of children were interned with their parents. Actually, hearing their shouts made us forget completely we were at war. I explained to her then that we were prisoners, too, and the nuns couldn't take care of children. But Anny wouldn't listen. She insisted over and over, and, to make us change our minds, she told us what her mother had heard about the treatment the Germans inflicted on the Jews in the camps. This is when I first heard about the unimaginable.

There were concentration camps, she said, where the Germans asked prisoners — old people, women and children — to take off all their clothes, making them think they were going to take a shower. Once they were locked inside the building, they were exterminated with a deadly gas.

At first this story seemed totally improbable to me and I didn't believe a word of it. It was impossible, beyond all understanding! I didn't want to hear anything more about it. I wanted to get away, I felt sick. I pulled myself together, grabbed my cousin's arm, and told the girl without even looking at her that we had to go and unfortunately couldn't help her.

We walked quickly toward the main building to join the other nuns. I didn't dare ask them if they had got wind of these horror stories, too. If Anny's story was true, I certainly didn't want to hear any others, so I would have the strength to live through this ordeal without the feeling of being a coward poisoning my thoughts on top of everything else. This evil was far too great for me.

In May, a rumour grew more persistent. People said that Canada demanded its citizens be returned. Good news at last! The authorities were taking care of us. A list of people to be set free was posted daily on the door of the commandant's office and we went to check it every morning. Whenever the name of a Canadian woman was on it, she was given a train ticket and left immediately for Canada. We would be happy for her. But since my name was never there, I would be down in the dumps again. I felt deep grief every time. My name never appeared on that list.

One morning in June, around nine, two men from the Gestapo entered our building to carry out a thorough search. They found my diary, leafed through it and took me away. They had come upon a song a Canadian prisoner had written about Hitler. I had unfortunately copied it down.

> Mr. Hitler, in his hellish brain,
> Dreamt up the plan one ill-fated day
> To shut all the British away,
> Without a murmur, their freedom gone,
> Just like that, at the break of dawn,
> In the barracks of Besançon.

Also scribbled down were a few comments on the way we were treated. I felt as though I was being arrested a second time. Yet I had known it was dangerous to keep a diary. The soldiers dragged me outside, treating me roughly, not even giving me a moment to say goodbye to my friends.

The train to Germany I was on left in the night. It was so crowded there was barely room to sit down. We were in boxcars and the smell was unbearable. I huddled up in a corner, using my habit as a mask to filter out the sickening odours.

On the journey that took me straight to hell, I never stopped blaming myself. No act of contrition could ever ease my remorse. I felt naive and irresponsible. Because I had continued to keep that cursed diary, I had just lost everything that was important to me, the only family I had ever known, the two nuns in whose company I had spent the past year. As time went by, they had become my lifeline. We felt truly close to each another, and it wasn't just because we were members of the same religious community. I looked upon them as my sisters, in the literal sense of the word. Reality hit me full in the face. From now on, I was alone in the world.

I cannot say how many hours the journey lasted because I lost all track of time. But when the train stopped, we were in Germany.

Third Notebook

Arrival at the Final Camp

I had just arrived at the camp where I would spend the next four years of my life. According to the women who were with me, we had travelled for five days and five nights.

Now, as I write this story, I still wonder how we managed to survive such a trip, locked in a boxcar. We needed an iron constitution. There was a tiny opening in the car's roof that let in fresh air. This air vent was covered with barbed wire, so it was impossible for a prisoner to stick his hand out and make his presence known. In the villages through which we travelled, no one would have had any idea there were people locked inside those boxcars.

I have no words to describe the foul stench filling the car. Added to body odours was the smell of death, because several people hadn't survived. They died on the way right beside us.

I was taken to the camp of Buchenwald, located in Thüringen, in Germany. My new address, for the next four years, would be Konzentrationlager Buchenwald. At the end of the war, I found out that this was a large industrial complex. We, the detainees, were used as labour for German industry. Buchenwald comprised several labour camps. There was among others a metal-appliances manufacturing plant, a brickyard, an aircraft factory, and a munitions factory. I had to work in this last one.

We were a group of about six hundred women, of various nationalities. First, we had to wait in line on a vast stretch of wasteland so the soldiers could take attendance. They shouted out our names in alphabetical order and our official numbers. I hoped that because of my nun status and the triviality of my offence, I had been misdirected and shouldn't be here. When I heard my name, distorted by the German accent, and my official number, 2074, I knew my last hope had just vanished into thin air. They handed me a time card that specified my place of work.

We had to stand and wait in the middle of that wasteland for three long hours. After all we had just been through in that hellish train, this was the last straw. Several women fainted. Others, still upright, tried to help them as best they could. I had dizzy spells and felt sick. But since I got out of the train, I was breathing much better and my stomach gradually settled. I tried to fight against the despair that overwhelmed me, but I couldn't even cry anymore, as though I were empty inside.

I was very worried, and wondered what life in that camp would be like. Some French prisoners who understood German had heard soldiers say they were taking us to that camp just to make us work in the armament factories. This reassured me. It struck me as odd, though, that there was no camp, or watch-tower, or barbed-wire fence anywhere in sight.

Also, I was intrigued by a railway track that disappeared behind two huge metal doors that were hidden from view by branches. It seemed a train could easily enter the building you could tell was behind those doors despite the forest camouflage.

To help the soldiers watch us, there were dogs dressed in little grey coats with the letters SS embroidered on the collars. At that time I still believed dogs couldn't be fundamentally vicious. But in those outfits they scared me as much as the soldiers did. Their getup even gave them a haughty look. I was immensely sad to see that the dogs, too, had been trained to feel no pity whatsoever toward human beings.

After roll call we were led to the entrance of the labour camp. Through a door that was also hidden behind a grassy, branch-covered hillock, we went down a staircase of about two hundred steps and ended up in a large room. There, we had to take off our clothes in front of the soldiers. Several girls, me being the first, refused. The dogs then started barking and we quickly realized we had no choice.

I had never undressed in front of anyone before. Needless to say I felt intensely embarrassed. I turned this way and that, stalling, not knowing what to do. A prisoner who noticed my distress came up to help me. Her name was Simone. She was from Quebec, too. She suggested I start with my underwear before taking off my robe. I wouldn't be naked for quite as long that way. I did what she said. First I took off my stockings, then my cotton undergarments, but as I began to remove my habit, I panicked and started to shake. Over and over I said that I couldn't.

A soldier walked toward me and ordered me in his language, which I didn't understand, to take off my clothes. He was just about to strike me with the butt of his rifle when Simone conveyed to him that she was going to take care of me. Fortunately, the soldier didn't hit me. Perhaps for a split second he felt some compassion because I was a nun. Simone said to me in a hushed voice, "You must realize that no one here has a choice, but I understand it isn't easy for you."

She had me raise my arms to take off my habit and then quickly put it in my hands so I could cover myself a little.

As soon as we were all naked, they began to shave us from head to toe. The women to whom this task had been assigned were prisoners, too. When my turn came, they had to wrench my habit from me. It felt as though the shield that protected me from the outside world was taken away, and I howled. Simone gripped my arm to make me stop screaming. In a low voice she told me to take deep breaths. She added, "While they shave you, try to think of something else and put all your energy into it."

But to feel the hands of a stranger crawling over my body was too much. Though I prayed to God with all my might, I couldn't calm down. I wasn't the only one in this position. Several girls struggled and they were beaten black and blue. I was lucky enough to have Simone by my side; she made me see reason. She kept telling me to breathe deeply and said there was nothing I could do anyway.

Having my head shaved didn't upset me because I already experienced this when I took my vows. Then they handed out clothes: a dress cut out of coarse cotton, which looked suspiciously like a flour sack open at both ends, as well as a pair of heavily worn ankle boots.

They made us line up in groups of four. Simone immediately positioned herself beside me. She probably thought I wasn't going to manage without her help, and she was quite right. Each group of four was given a badly dented mess bowl so rusty it turned your stomach. Simone volunteered to go and fetch our portion. She came back with a half-full bowl. We took turns sipping a thick, greyish soup that smelled awful.

Next, they led us to what they called the toilets, a most disheartening sight. Before us was a large, empty, low-ceilinged room. At its centre lay very long, rectangular slabs of concrete with a double row of holes in them. To relieve ourselves, we had to sit down on the cement, side by side and back to back, without any partitions to give us privacy. At first glance, the number of cavities was far from sufficient for our group, and the openings were already soiled with the excrements of women who had sat on them before us. The fetid smell caught so violently in our throats that several of us threw up the revolting stew we had just swallowed.

These poor sanitary conditions contributed to the rapid spread of germs. Some women's backsides were covered with spots; they suffered from vitamin deficiency and various infections. Moreover, there was no toilet paper. A corner of that room had a wash basin with a tap that only let out a thin trickle of water. This wash basin was completely inadequate for the personal hygiene of about six hundred women.

Since we no longer had any underwear, we gradually realized we would be unable to sponge up our menstrual blood, which made the premises even more unhealthy. Several girls, myself included, began to cry out of sheer powerlessness in the face of implacable fate. I never thought that in a single day I would be so dehumanized and terrified and that my chastity would be violated.

We then made our way toward the spot where a few hours later we would start our hard work. The soldiers showed us what our tasks would be. The underground camp where we had ended up was used, among other things, for the production of ammunition for rifles, submachine guns, machine guns, mines, and tanks.

In rooms next to ours, prisoners made aircraft parts and wiring. The women worked on the smaller parts. We found out a little later that the men were assigned to the manufacture of bigger armament parts and worked two floors down.

Connected with the large central room were several small galleries. In one of these, women made cartridges. This place was farther away because of the explosion risk. There was a mine-production workshop. In one of the rooms, inmates melted down and cast metal. I also saw impressive sewing machines, which were used for making belts and straps that would hold bullets for machine guns. My job, in fact, was going to consist in fastening the ammunition to those belts and straps.

The place was surreal. You would think you were in an underground city. Because of the thickness of the concrete walls, we couldn't hear what went on in the other rooms, and even less what was happening outside. We were so far below ground we didn't even notice air raids anymore. This struck me as odd because air raids had been part of my everyday life since my arrest. At first I jumped whenever I heard the whistling of bombs that had just been dropped. I was afraid I was going to die. In time, my panic faded, but my fear of dying remained. So there was a positive side to this underground camp: Since I no longer heard the blasts of the explosions, I no longer wondered how many casualties the next bomb was going to cause.

The soldiers then showed us a so-called infirmary. Red crosses had been painted on the two doors that barred the entrance. Trespassers were severely punished. We would find out a few weeks later that it was also the antechamber of death. When there were too many wounded and it was necessary to make room, the soldiers didn't hesitate to select the weakest among the prisoners and put them to death. Thus, male and female inmates suffering from either slight or serious malformations were taken to the "infirmary" and never came back. A mere facial paralysis or abnormal hairiness in a woman was enough to make her disappear. Also, women who couldn't accept being imprisoned and wasted away before our very eyes, were inevitably sent there, on the pretext that they were no longer able to work. After soldiers had slashed the women's wrists, they let them bleed to death, and then claimed that the women had committed suicide. This was just a fraction of what went on behind those doors.

Our tour of the premises seemed never-ending and completely undermined what little morale we had left. Simone and I walked arm in arm so we could help each other to put one foot in front of the other. We were exhausted. The soldiers finally took us to the room where we would sleep. There were four dormitories, designated with letters A through D. Simone and I ended up in B.

We were all assigned á straw mattress, which badly needed fresh straw, one for every four women. The only bedding we were given was a black, rough-textured blanket, and it would have to be shared by four of us. The place reeked of sweat, dirt, and damp. Our makeshift bed was off to the side, and we met the other two women who were going to share our blanket. Mathilde Perret introduced herself. She was French, but wouldn't tell us why she had been detained. We didn't press her. She was a very beautiful woman, aloof, severe-looking, with an erect posture, blue-green eyes, and fine features. Tall and slim, she must have caught the eye of many men. Even without hair, as thin as she had become and in that ugly dress, she attracted the soldiers' attention. Just the opposite of Simone, who radiated genuine good-heartedness. She was somewhat on the short side, like me, with a plump figure she unfortunately lost, and had hazel eyes similar to mine. She had been arrested for the same reason as me, guilty of being a British subject. She had married a Breton but had kept her Canadian citizenship. "Had I known!..." she often said to me.

The other woman, Iréna, was Polish. She only knew a few words of French. We didn't know the reason for her arrest. She was a frail young girl, brown-haired, with a delicate face. Her turquoise blue eyes made us uneasy when she watched us. It struck me right away, as soon as I saw her, that she needed to be protected, like a small, wounded animal. She was withdrawn and obviously didn't trust us.

How can you avoid forging close bonds when you share a mattress? But the atmosphere wasn't conducive to friendship for the moment.

Before I went to sleep, I kneeled down and, with my face to the ground, I said over and over, "It's your own fault you have ended up here. The others *did* warn you not to hold on to your diary!"

All of a sudden Simone gently took my hand and said, "We are all going to suffer a lot here. You don't need to hurt yourself on top of it."

Thanks to Simone's comforting presence, I calmed down and finally fell asleep, curled up against her back. From that day on, we were inseparable.

Everyday Life at the Camp

At half past four in the morning, the shrill sound of a whistle wakened us. All the women got up, and we had to wait for the group from dormitory A to come back from the toilets before we could rush in there. In the early morning, the bad smells seemed worse to me than the night before. I felt nauseous. Several of us were sick even before entering.

We tried to wash, but the wait was so long and the trickle of water so thin that it was impossible. We would try again another day, especially since we shouldn't run the risk of being late for work. Any lateness was considered a serious offence, liable to attract a harsh penalty.

I suffered greatly from the lack of hygiene. The Germans treated us like animals, but unfortunately *we* couldn't lick ourselves clean. I often said to myself that I wouldn't be able to inflict such a fate on my worst enemy. We then made it our objective to find soap. Soap and food became our two priorities.

When we returned to the dormitories, the soldier on guard started the count and took attendance again. On the very first day, a girl whose straw mattress was within a few paces of ours, died. Iréna, the Polish girl, then slipped in beside her and, taking advantage of the fact that the guard had his back to us, held her in an upright position. When the soldier shouted out the dead prisoner's name to give her her portion, Iréna yelled "present" in her place and so was able to collect the dead woman's bread ration. She then laid the lifeless body on the ground and immediately crept back to us. We were in shock and stunned by Iréna's behaviour. How could such a delicate-looking girl be strong enough to lift up a corpse so quickly?

What we didn't know at the time was that she had been imprisoned in another camp before ending up with us. So she knew all the tricks to secure her survival.

But the three other girls who shared their straw mattress with the deceased glared at Iréna when they realized the consequence of what she had done. They were dumbfounded to see someone near them stealing the bread portion of a girl who had died on their own mattress.

That first morning, after swallowing our meagre allotment of gruel and our small piece of grey bread, we assembled so we could be divided into work parties. I was shown the machine I would work with for the next four years; until my liberation in fact.

My work consisted in fixing aircraft machine-gun bullets to a belt, which was called a "braid." This was extremely dangerous work. If ever the fixing mechanism wasn't properly aligned and I still pushed the pedal, the wire that pressed against the bullet might well cause an explosion because of the exerted pressure. One moment's inattention and I could have killed or seriously injured myself. I felt as though I were handling actual bombs.

I had no choice: I needed to concentrate on my work. I was utterly surprised, therefore, to hear the whistle announcing the midday break. I hadn't noticed the morning going by, and the afternoon passed just as quickly. Yet we had to work for twelve hours! I made every effort not to injure myself. Without realizing it, I was putting into practice what Simone had advised me to do: "Keep your mind occupied when you suffer; it will be less painful."

But there were moments in the late afternoon when I had trouble keeping my eyes open. Waving my hand about over and over again, I would ask permission to go to the toilets. I would splash cold water on my face. This had the desired effect, and, while I was there, I drank lots of water. Revived, I could carry on until six. There was hardly anyone at the wash basin at that time. Perhaps the other women were too embarrassed to ask, but I dared. The worst that could happen was that I'd be turned down.

During evening attendance and roll call, we were forced to stand stock-still. This procedure could take two hours. Several of us were exhausted and had to be helped by others to remain upright. I always wondered why this operation was repeated morning and night, since no one could possibly escape from the camp. One day, Mathilde told me the reason. The day's dead needed to be counted mainly to avoid wasting food … ·

For the evening meal, the term "ration" was used: three centimetres of bread the same colour as that of the morning, sometimes mouldy, with a dab of margarine, and, once a week, a spoonful of marmalade.

I didn't notice at first that I was losing weight because there were no mirrors. But we saw our fellow prisoners becoming skin and bone. We tried any way we could to find a little more food. In this, we weren't very far from Iréna's philosophy. We were prepared to do anything for a piece of bread.

In the first week, Simone volunteered to go and get the gruel pot from the kitchens. It took four women to carry it, two in front and two behind, because even empty, the pot was too heavy for one woman.

Eventually a soldier noticed Simone's repeated volunteering to help out at mealtime. After several weeks she became an employee. The SS chose personnel from among the prisoners to do the routine work they would otherwise have to carry out themselves. To some, they delegated certain administrative and supply duties. These women worked in the offices, warehouses, kitchens, and infirmaries. Simone was assigned to the kitchen.

A few weeks later, Mathilde was selected, too, and put in charge of supplies. This was an important job, which she got mainly because she spoke German quite well.

Thanks to her new position, Simone was allowed to go into the kitchens and managed to bring us more bread, or a small potato. One day she brought us a piece of sausage she had stolen, wrapped in an old dish towel.

She felt guilty at first for sharing these little treats just with the three of us. Mathilde quickly brought her back to reality: "Listen, if we grow stronger thanks to your little leftovers, we'll be able to help more girls to get through this."

Get through this! Some of us were beginning to think we would never survive this hell. Luckily, we, the four girls on our mattress, constituted a solid unit and that kept us from being too depressed. Little by little, we began to form a kind of wall of resistance, which stayed upright thanks to our complementary strengths.

Every night before going to sleep, we talked about what had happened during the day. If one of us had felt a pang of despair, she would no longer be alone to bear it: the three others would take on a share of it. If I survived all of that horror, it is largely thanks to Simone, Mathilde, and Iréna. These three admirable women taught me to be strong. They communicated their fighting spirit to me and encouraged me to be resilient.

The women who entered the camp while repeating over and over, "We are going to die here," nearly all died at the camp. Those, however, who kept saying, "They won't get us. We are going to come out of this place alive!" mostly survived.

Here is the portrait of these women with whom I lived through the worst times of my life.

SIMONE

As soon as we arrived at the camp, I realized she had unbelievable strength of character. She glared at the Germans in a way that would have made the most hardened of torturers quake in his boots. At the same time she was the embodiment of goodness, never indifferent to the fate of others. She shouldered the responsibility for our four stomachs. All day long, the only thing on her mind was our dietary survival and she would try to find small compensations to make our everyday life a little more pleasant.

Once, she managed to steal some pieces of cardboard from the kitchen, which she hid under her dress, one at a time. She then put them under our straw mattress to block the damp rising from the concrete.

Born in Trois-Rivières, Simone married a Breton, Léon Bocage. He was her Léon, as she used to say to us.

Léon had met Simone, a friend of his sister-in-law, on a trip to Montreal, where he had gone to visit his brother, Paul. The two Bocage brothers had inherited the family patisserie, in the village of Hédé, twenty-four kilometres from Rennes, in Brittany. Paul decided to let his brother have the business and settled in North America.

Simone was twenty-five when she met Léon. He was twenty-nine. In a few days, they became inseparable. Being single, unattached, she dropped everything to follow him to Europe.

They got married, and were working together in the family patisserie when they were arrested. Léon closed the shop on the day of his arrest. The Germans were aware of his reputation as a pastry cook and forced him to come and work in the kitchens of the German army's headquarters in Rennes. Léon suspected that sooner or later Simone, still a Canadian citizen and therefore a British subject, was going to be arrested, too. The couple knew a lot about the war, thanks to all the customers who came into their shop. Before he left, Léon made Simone swear she would try everything to survive this war, and he promised he would do the same.

I could understand why Léon loved Simone because, since I met her, Simone had been my rock. I was in great need of her kindness and resourcefulness. I felt safe with her. She had become my older sister. I always sought her approval before carrying out anything at all. With her sense of humour she was often able to make the day's events seem less alarming.

It took an awfully long while, though, before we could laugh again. The first few times we managed to smile were mainly Simone's doing. To make fun of the soldiers, she would call them "those nice guys." She had even come up with a code to warn of impending danger. Being a pastry cook, she decided that "charlotte russe" would be a really good password to alert us. But two words, that was much too long, and we unanimously chose "charlotte."

Nearly every mattress had its code, in fact. As soon as someone spotted a soldier coming too near us, prisoners were heard whispering names of colours, numbers, and so on.

Simone occupied such a large place in our lives that when she was down in the dumps, we were affected by it, too. We would be eager for her to recover her high spirits, her sparkle, and black humour. Her sin of gluttony became, for us, an asset. Yes, Simone was very fond of her food and often took great risks to hunt up treasures for us, snatched straight from the officers' dishes.

If we were sharing a carrot, Simone would say, "Just think, girls, that a carrot is often cooked along with a chicken in a sauce, or with a beef stew, and it can be mashed with potatoes." Our mouths would water and, with our eyes closed, we slowly savoured our quarter of the carrot. Both being Quebeckers,

Simone and I salivated most at the thought of the beef stew. For Iréna, it was the purée, and all Mathilde could think of was the chicken.

MATHILDE

Mathilde, the Resistance fighter. The mysterious, elusive one. Mental strength personified. She never wasted words and always thought before she spoke.

She spent most of her time observing, analyzing, and finding clever ways to cheat, to distract the soldiers' attention. Endowed with a phenomenal memory, she knew all the guards' schedules by heart, since she couldn't write anything down.

She was able to memorize the face of every soldier who watched us, and had the gift of picking out the most humane among them. She had a good grasp of the basics of the German language and often asked us to be quiet to better hear the soldiers' conversations.

Before the shaving session, her hair was golden blond. Judging by the clothes she wore when she arrived at the camp, she must have been a very elegant woman before her imprisonment. She no doubt owed her job in the camp's administrative services to her great physical appeal.

Her work consisted in drawing up inventories of certain products manufactured here. Her relationship with the officers was therefore on a different level.

Mathilde was arrested in Nancy, her birthplace, because she was a member of the Resistance. She taught history. The Germans arrested her in her lycée.

She was single and went to see her parents every Sunday. One day, when rumours of the Second World War began to circulate in earnest, her father, who had fought in the First World War, changed completely. The looming conflict became his only topic of conversation. Before a part of France was occupied, Mathilde took little interest in political issues and thought her father was a lovable but silly old fool. She began to listen carefully to him, though, when she heard that Paris had become an "open city" and the Germans moved around freely there. Then she started asking questions.

One day, a friend of her father's, a Jewish woman of Alsatian origin who had been their neighbour from the very beginning, shot herself in the head. She had left a letter to explain why she did it. The prospect of falling into the hands of the Nazi invaders was unbearable to her. Jewish friends had told her that members of their family had disappeared. Many horror stories were beginning to surface. Hitler hadn't yet given the order to exterminate the Jewish people, but the Dachau and Auschwitz camps already existed. That neighbour had heard enough and knew she wouldn't have the strength to survive such brutal treatment. The suicide confronted Mathilde with harsh reality. She was deeply shaken, and her father inconsolable. It was above all the thought of this woman that made her decide to act.

Little by little, her apartment became a political haven. Her colleagues from the lycée who wished to be involved by working in the *armée des ombres*, as the friends of the Resistance were called, would meet at her home. If before joining the movement she had been unconvinced her co-workers could make a difference in this conflict, she now realized the importance of small acts.

First of all, she learned the enemy's language, the most frequently used words at least. Her role consisted in circulating information. She would go to public places, and, sometimes without uttering a single word, exchange a piece of information or a code word hidden inside a newspaper. She knew the risk she ran, but felt relieved no one asked her to take part in what was commonly called "horizontal collaboration." That was the term used for women who granted sexual favours to the Germans in exchange for information, food, or to actually save someone's life. These women must have had no reservations of a moral nature. They were doing "their part" in that way to help the Resistance, as a last resort.

Later, Mathilde was one of these women. Because she made that sacrifice, we were eventually able to emerge from the darkness.

IRÉNA

Darkness. The perfect word to describe Iréna, the ultimate survivor. Iréna possessed both the innocence of a child and an extraordinary instinct for survival. She could endure suffering without uttering a word. That was her greatest strength. It is around her that we erected our stronghold. Iréna deserved more than anyone else to make it through. I knew very well that the ability to stay alive had nothing to do with merit, but having her survive the horror was a victory over infamy for us and gave meaning to the years we wasted in that hole. Since life had not been kind to her, we hoped that one day she would know a different fate. Born in Poznán, in Poland, Iréna shared a small apartment in that city with her mother and younger sister. The SS cavalry regularly conducted roundups there. They would take the Jews from their homes and beat them up or kill them in the middle of the street. Her father was arrested in one of the first of these roundups. Iréna never saw him again. She and some friends decided to go into hiding in the country, at an uncle's house, until everything, they thought, got back to normal and the violence ended.

After a few weeks in the country, where she wasn't worried and ate particularly well, Iréna made up her mind to go back to the city, thinking the danger had passed. It was the feast day of St. Irène, her birthday. She was twenty-one and hoped her mother would give a party for her. Her mother wasn't at home, but Iréna decided to make preparations for a party, anyway.

Her mother and sister were at the community garden, at the other end of town. Suddenly the SS burst into the apartment and asked her if she knew if her family was hiding Jews whose status was illegal. Iréna answered there was no one hidden in her house. The soldiers were furious. They proceeded to turn the whole apartment upside down. One SS man showed her some photographs and asked her if she knew these people. Afraid her family would suffer reprisals, Iréna chose to keep silent. The soldiers then decided to cart her off. As she went down the building's narrow stairs ahead of them, she passed her mother and sixteen-year-old sister, who were just coming back. They both looked at her, wondering what was happening. Iréna discreetly signalled to them to ignore her. Her mother began to cry softly, holding her other daughter's hand very tightly. They passed right by their apartment so as not to attract the soldiers' attention.

The SS men took Iréna to their headquarters and tried to make her sign certain papers. Iréna refused, saying she didn't understand their language. She was then sent to the town's prison. Her mother came to see her a little later. She gave her a blanket and a cushion: "You can sit on it if it's too cold on the floor or if you have a backache."

Iréna stayed at another camp before coming to this last one. The first, Auschwitz, established in 1940, included two separate complexes: Auschwitz-Birkenau, the extermination camp, and Auschwitz-Monowitz, the labour camp, where she was taken. The first three days after her arrest, she cried a lot. She felt completely numb for a while, as though she were observing from the outside what she experienced within. We all felt that way at one time or another.

While there, she escaped death thanks to a woman prisoner from her hometown. An SS leader had decided on a whim to send all those Jews to the crematorium whose identification number tattooed on their arms contained the figure *seven*. Iréna's number was 24215. The figure *one* had been tattooed with a longer line at the top, so that it looked like a *seven*. Consequently, Iréna ended up among the detainees who were going to be sent to the crematorium.

The woman prisoner who dealt with the registers of the camp's inmates knew Iréna. She went to see the officer right away and proved to him that it wasn't a *seven* Iréna had her on her arm because the figure lacked the little cross stroke it often has in Europe. The SS checked the register, saw there had been a mistake, and Iréna was spared.

When she arrived in our camp, she was rather distrustful. But little by little, as we showed her affection, her distrust disappeared. She was the last one to share her story and even let us see her official number tattooed on her arm. That was risky because it was due to a mix-up while being transferred that she had ended up with us. She became a treasure we needed to protect at all cost. We made sure her tattoo was always well covered up by a layer of mud, which we made with water, sand and any dirt we found under our boots. When a soldier came too near her, we would try to divert his attention in every possible way.

Mathilde became her guardian angel. She used all her power to obtain certain well-deserved advantages for Iréna and made that her personal business.

Through her intervention, for example, Iréna was given other work because the work she had been doing, the packing of arms, was too exhausting.

What should be pointed out is that there existed a hierarchy among prisoners. Mathilde, who was French and spoke German, was at the top of the ladder. Then came Simone and I, two British subjects. At the bottom of the scale were all the others, except the Jews, who were unclassifiable. So, thanks to Mathilde, Iréna was assigned to another, less physically demanding job and found herself, like me, assembling belts for machine-gun bullets. With the consent of two officers, Mathilde managed throughout our captivity to leave Iréna's name out of the Lottery of Death.

Special Days

At the camp, we lost all track of time. Our only reference point was the day of Hitler's birthday, April 20, because then we were entitled to a slice of sausage. How generous of him! That's how I could tell how many years I had been locked up here.

Gradually a certain routine settled in, in spite of the horror around us. The production of arms seemed to be our guards' main concern. In the course of my second year of captivity, however, the German soldiers started behaving more violently toward us. There must have been a reason. At the beginning of the war, Mathilde said, the German army was confident it would win. But the situation had become more difficult, owing to the huge loss of life on the battlefields. The troops' morale was affected by this. It was out of the question for Hitler to suffer another defeat like the one of 1914–18.

One day, after our shift and roll call, the soldiers decided to make up a new game to avenge themselves for the deaths of their countrymen killed in action. They would place the prisoners' names in the helmet of a soldier and the woman whose name was drawn was shot on the spot, in front of all the others. We called this appalling game the "Lottery of Death." It took place once a month.

How can I describe the dread they made us endure while we waited for them to draw the name of the woman who would be doomed to die? We would stand close together. When we heard that our name hadn't been chosen, we couldn't help but be relieved, but at the same time we felt immensely sad for the woman who was going to be shot.

When the soldier took aim at the prisoner and she began to scream, we turned around so we wouldn't have to witness that horrible scene. It was unspeakable. The screams of those girls have always haunted my sleep. Yet the height of barbarism hadn't been reached yet.

There were twins among us, just eighteen years old. They were from Quebec. They happened to be in Brittany when they were arrested. Their father, an engineer, had been awarded a two-year contract for the building of a bridge and decided to take his little family with him. On a certain day, a soldier drew the name of one of the twins. Her sister started howling and clung to her. The girls who shared their mattress tried to hold her back, but when the gun went off and her sister fell, she cried and screamed even louder. As no one was able to calm her down, the soldier ordered the girls to stand back with the tip of his gun and then fired at the other twin, who collapsed on top of her sister, who was already dead.

This time, we didn't have a chance to turn around and we saw it all. We never expected such an inhuman act. The soldier himself seemed surprised by his impulsive decision. He was no longer able to look us in the eye. I had a feeling that the soldiers found our distress so difficult to bear that their rage turned them into real beasts. Perhaps they wanted to indicate to us that they really had no choice but to act this way, they were just following orders and couldn't do anything about it. Otherwise, they might go mad …

Another ordeal was repeated every month to try and make us feel inferior and dehumanize us, as though the soldiers wanted to prove to the enemy that if we didn't surrender to Germany, they would continue ill-treating us. Yet we were only enemy ants, hidden three hundred feet underground. We couldn't serve as an example to anyone. The acts of cruelty they committed toward us showed their frustration at not winning the war as easily as they thought they would.

We believed that certain soldiers made it their mission to think up new forms of torture, just to impress their *Führer*.

So, once a month, our guards forced us to walk past them naked while they pointed at us and made fun of us. Their loud, coarse laughter still rings in my ears.

Sometimes during this parade, carried out in front of two officers and a group of soldiers, girls had their period. That made them laugh even more. Fortunately, my menstrual cycle had stopped since my arrest (which caused me many problems later on). Be that as it may, it meant one humiliation less for me. Mathilde was our guide and made her recommendations. She told us to hold ourselves very erect and, especially, always look the voyeurs in the eye, without blinking. At the end of this degrading procession, several girls had no strength left to go on. Their distress was so unbearable that we often heard a few of them scream that they wanted to die and needed our help to kill themselves. As for our group of four, it became even more closely knit, and we were convinced we were going to survive. Improbable as it may seem, we were confident and defiant. Our passion for life was so strong that all we wanted to do was spit on every German.

Toward the end of the second year, punishments began to rain on us for anything and everything. A bowl not put back where it belonged, a crooked row at roll call, being a minute late for work; anything was an excuse to penalize us. That might mean a few days of solitary confinement, with or without light, a soup ration only once every four days, or spending time in a cell that was flooded up to your ankles.

Occasionally our guards forced prisoners to punish each other. One day, a Russian woman tried to escape but didn't succeed. The three inmates who shared her mattress were punished. For two and a half days they had to remain standing, a sanction the soldiers called "the pose." This was followed by three days of food deprivation. Next, rather than dealing with the fugitive themselves, the guards handed her over to her fellow inmates so they would punish her. Then the girls beat her to death! The Germans really knew all the ways to turn human beings into brutes.

I have also had experiences that were unusual to say the least, especially considering the situation I was in: While busy working one morning, I thought I heard someone speak to me in a hushed voice. The staple machine was making a noise and I couldn't quite make out where the sound of that voice came from. Anyway, I carried on with my work.

Then, once again, between two pedal strokes, I heard someone whisper beside me. Incredible as it may seem, a young soldier on guard duty was trying to talk to me. This struck me as so unbelievable that at first I thought I wasn't in my right mind. But on his way back, the soldier slowed down to be closer to my work station. "It's *me* talking to you. Hello!" As he walked past me again, he said hello to me once more. This time I knew for sure who was speaking to me. I was stunned, it was beyond all comprehension.

I lowered my eyes as though nothing had happened. I couldn't answer him; after all, it could be a trick. If I opened my mouth, there would certainly be dreadful consequences. He must have noticed my confusion because he tried to reassure me: "I don't mean to frighten you. I would just like to chat with you, only if you want to, of course."

The idea of chatting with a torturer seemed diabolical, so naturally I hesitated. He went on, "I am not who you think

I am. I assure you this isn't a trap. I know perfectly well we could both suffer grave reprisals, but I can't help it. I have been watching you for the past few days and seen such strength of character in you that I wanted to talk to you so I could find out a little more about you. I was anxious to tell you that I am very unhappy about what is going on at the moment. I am not trying to justify myself. I simply wanted to say that not all Germans agree with this war. I would especially like to explain that not all of us are heartless men. If you decide to speak to me, we'll be extremely careful. We'll talk without moving our mouths too much and without looking at each other. I cannot trust anyone either because some soldiers are very indoctrinated and denounce the most humane among us. If it will reassure you: I have thoroughly weighed the risks. For example, the position of the stapler you work with makes it easier to communicate because it's at quite a distance from the other guards. From where I am, I have a clear view of the entrance stairway. When I suspect danger or feel we are being watched, I will stop talking immediately for your safety and mine."

And he continued, without asking if I agreed, "All right then, I'll begin, Mademoiselle. My name is Franz. I am sure you are wondering why I am speaking to you in French. That is because I received part of my education in Paris. I lived there for two years."

I didn't even look at him. I was really afraid it might be a trap. A few moments after the whistle that marked the end of the shift had sounded, he said, "See you tomorrow!"

I was in a state of shock.

At night I waited for the eight o'clock curfew and for all the lights to be switched off to tell my story to the girls. Pressed against each other — Simone at the end of the row, I next to her, Iréna and Mathilde at the other end — I whispered my conversation with the soldier to them.

Simone and Iréna warned me right away. "You must never trust the enemy," they said over and over. Neither one believed in the German soldier's benevolence. "There must be something he wants from you," they said. "You believed him when he explained he spoke to you because he admired your strength of character?" Mathilde asked, and added, "We'll have to protect you, not just from soldiers but men in general."

I couldn't quite understand what she meant by that. The three of them insisted that I stop these exchanges immediately.

The following morning, as soon as she got up, Simone reminded me once again of their instructions. If that soldier happened to be still on guard duty today, I should ignore him. I didn't promise anything, but I agreed just to get rid of her and went to my work station. Franz was still on guard. Strangely enough, I felt a peculiar little rush of joy when I caught sight of him. Was that only because he took an interest in me?

Franz waited patiently until we were all back at our posts and the steady noise of the machines started up again before he tried to approach me. I took advantage of the moments when he wasn't looking at me to observe him. I took my time examining him. He was blond, with eyes too blue to be mean, fine features, large hands. I jumped when he said hello to me. He told me his name again and asked for mine. I didn't answer. He tried to put me at ease. "I understand perfectly why you keep silent, after what you have been through. I am going to tell you my story and then you will decide if I am worthy of your attention."

While I carried on with my work and without ever looking at him, I listened to him describing himself.

"My name is Franz Weis. I come from Garmisch-Partenkirchen, near the Austrian border, in Bavaria. Those two villages were amalgamated in 1935 on Hitler's orders, in anticipation of the Olympic Games of 1936. Garmisch lies in a magnificent valley surrounded by mountains. One of these, the Zugspitze, is the tallest in Germany. If you can come to visit this place one day, you'll see how pretty it is.

"In my family, we have been soldiers for three generations. My father fought in the First World War. He is a very cold person. In his opinion, a man should never show his feelings. You can imagine it was out of the question that his son would avoid his military service. I don't know if he is proud of my getting my degree in history in Paris, because he never told me. I feel I will never accomplish enough for him to look at me with pride. That's why I hate him sometimes.

. "Paris is an enthralling city. The two years that I lived there were the most rewarding years of my life. I fell deeply in love with the city and my only wish, once this terrible war is over, if I get out of it alive of course, is to go back and live there and become a journalist."

Franz got carried away as he told his story. He forgot to speak in a low voice. He asked me, "Have you been there?" He didn't know how badly I wanted to answer, but I did nothing of the sort. "Fine. Don't answer me. I understand."

He continued: "It is a fascinating, elegant and romantic city, because of the architecture, the wide avenues, the vast parks. I keep thinking back to my strolls on the Champs-Élysées, in the late afternoon. It was magical. The trees lining the avenue are extremely well looked after. There are many cafés where you can enjoy a good café au lait while watching the women with their elegant clothes and the impeccably dressed men. There is also the Place de la Concorde and the obelisk given to the city by the Egyptians, the Bois de Boulogne, the Eiffel Tower with its astonishing metal structure we have all heard so much about since the World's Fair. I lived in a small *pension*, on rue Washington, in a beautiful neighbourhood. I went to see *Carmen* at the Opéra-Comique. I saw the musée Grévin and its wax figures. Those are unique experiences. To live in Paris means to be surrounded by art and science. Paris thrills me. When I lived there, I felt elated and eagerly looked forward to the future."

I was just about to answer when an officer very nearly caught us. Franz suddenly stopped talking. He hadn't heard him coming.

❖ ❖ ❖

That night, once we had settled ourselves on our straw mattress, Simone and Iréna lost no time in asking me if I had spoken to the soldier. I told them there had been no communication between us. I wondered why I felt the need to hide the truth from them.

I examined my conscience, asked myself when I last told a lie. I had no recollection of it because I am not accustomed to lying. It seems to me I have always been direct and frank. It's true that the life I had led until then encouraged that attitude.

I certainly didn't want the girls to lecture me. I had my pride, after all. But something else drove me to keep what was happening secret. There was this strange small fire that had just flared up within me.

I asked myself lots of questions and had trouble falling asleep. What could he have found so interesting in me that he chose me to chat with? It wasn't the first time a soldier tried to communicate with prisoners. In Besançon, when I distributed medicines at night with the nun from my congregation, I often encountered soldiers on guard duty who tried to talk to us. They, too, must have wanted to tell us that not all Germans were bastards, and they were only obeying orders.

Franz made me look for the first time at the other side of the picture. I had never wondered since my arrest if, among the soldiers we saw every day, there might be any who hated their situation. There were bound to be. Franz was probably not alone. I was inclined to give him the benefit of the doubt and thought to myself there had to be some Germans who disagreed, as he did, with what was happening. The soldiers also had mothers and women who loved them, who feared for their lives and worried about them, like all women the world over. I came to the conclusion that there is a bit of humanity in people from every country.

When Franz told me he had been watching me for a while, I was thrown into confusion. It seemed hard to believe. Try as I might, I couldn't recall a single instance of him observing me or his eyes meeting mine, even for a moment. I thought I would have remembered his bright blue eyes.

❖ ❖ ❖

I was perfectly aware that a bond was forming, but why should I have felt guilty? It was just a friendly conversation, after all. For me, this contact was balm on the concentration camp's ugliness and suffering. Gradually my mind filled with pleasant memories that helped me chase away the atrocities I had seen since I came to the camp. I was baffled by how quickly extreme cruelty could give way to hope.

All this soul-searching prevented me from falling asleep, although the day's work had been exhausting. I actually no longer felt tired.

That evening, Simone, Iréna, and I stayed awake for a good part of the night. Mathilde hadn't joined us on the mattress yet. It was the second time this happened. The first time, she merely told us not to worry, everything was fine. But there was such coldness in her explanation that we didn't dare ask questions. Perhaps she would tell us the reason for her absence later.

I finally stopped worrying about Mathilde and started to endlessly go over the past day in my mind. The night suddenly seemed too long to me and I was anxious for dawn to come so I could see Franz again.

Fourth Notebook

The Beginning

I hadn't seen Franz for two days now and I was worried. Had he been seen talking to me? Had something serious happened to him? While I worked, I constantly watched the entrance stairway in hopes of seeing him appear. I couldn't make sense of the way I felt about someone I had only met twice and, what's more, who was in the enemy camp. It was totally absurd. He was a German soldier whom I didn't know and couldn't trust. And yet I felt a great void, as though I had just lost a new friend, someone I would have wanted to know everything about and converse with as long as possible.

What had caused me to become so wrapped up in him? These feelings also seemed complicated to me because there was something other than mere friendship in what I felt for him. I knew nothing about the attraction between a man and a woman. Would I have had the same feelings for another man who would have paid as much attention to me as Franz? In any event, it wasn't really the right time to experience something like this.

I tried to dismiss Franz from my thoughts. I had great difficulty concentrating on my work. Yet I needed to. I couldn't afford a single mistake. A week or two before, a bullet had exploded in the face of a girl who was performing the same task because she hadn't fastened it properly to the machine-gun belt.

It was awful. She was completely disfigured. A few girls tried to help her, but we only had dirty cloths. She was screaming and we were powerless to do anything for her. The soldiers took her to the hospital and we never saw that girl again.

Some women told us the infection had spread quickly. The girl was unconscious. The soldiers then transported her to some other location to kill her. For a long time I remembered that girl with the disfigured face, and I was always afraid of suffering the same fate.

I worked half-heartedly; I was absorbed in my inner struggle, telling myself over and over that I shouldn't be affected by Franz. To convince myself, I impressed upon my mind that I couldn't become attached to someone I would never see again. Before I knew him, I was only just beginning to get used to the idea that I would be imprisoned for a long time and would need a great deal of courage and, above all, energy to keep my hatred strong. I didn't want to relent before the enemy, especially as the other soldiers were totally unlike him.

I wanted to hold on to my fighting spirit so that one day I would be able to spit in their faces and shout, "You won't get me. I am going to come out of this place alive!"

I wondered if Franz was an exception to this whole abomination, the proof that a human being can be fundamentally good. If so, that would be a ray of hope for me, and I needed it to endure the confinement. If by chance I never saw him again, I would still at the very least have my memory of him, while waiting for the day when I would be free.

I absolutely didn't want my friends to notice my melancholy mood, so I was very careful when I joined them at bedtime. I nonetheless spent part of the night probing my feelings for Franz.

❖ ❖ ❖

One evening an unusual event kept me awake. Krystina, a Polish woman, occupied the mattress next to ours. She had been arrested for some obscure reason, like all the other girls at the camp, and arrived here at the same time as her husband. He had been taken to the men's section.

Seven months pregnant, Krystina was doubled up with pain, but it was too early to give birth to the baby. For Simone, who often assisted her mother, a midwife, it was almost normal that labour had already started because of the harsh living conditions at the camp. She had also lost a lot of weight. For the past two months or so, we had taken turns at doing her work so she could rest as much as possible. In spite of our efforts there were complications. She was racked by strong contractions. One after the other, we tried to warm her up and comfort her. We didn't want to send her to the infirmary too soon, since she would be alone there. Simone wrapped Krystina in an old woollen jacket she had stolen from the kitchens.

We kept Krystina with us as long as we could. Then, in the middle of the night, we helped her along to the infirmary. Simone stayed with her until she gave birth a few minutes later to a beautiful little girl, called Inga, in honour of her best Polish friend.

We were worn out. It was only about half an hour before wake-up time and I felt sad, dejected. So I began my day in an utterly exhausted state. I walked to the spot where I worked, hanging my head listlessly. Franz's absence for the past few days made me feel even worse.

I avoided glancing around for fear of being disappointed once more, and concentrated on my machine. Then, at a certain point, unexpectedly, my eyes met Franz's. My tiredness vanished instantly. I had been so afraid I would never see him again that I decided that day to speak to him. Franz seemed happy to see me, too. He told me he had been asked to translate some texts and had worked in the headquarters' offices for two days.

Before making up my mind to talk to him, I performed one last examination of conscience, like any good nun. Well, for what remained of the nun in me. Was my intuition right? Was this a good man? Since he first spoke to me, I had never felt he was lying. Even though I hadn't associated with many human beings in my young convent life, I thought I had a talent for sensing if someone was good or bad. The nuns had often congratulated me on my instinct, in fact.

I knew all about the risk I ran, but could the penalty be any more atrocious than what I had been going through since I arrived at this camp? I realized that my bedmates would disagree with what I was about to do. In their opinion, the Germans were hypocrites and we shouldn't put our trust in them. I was stubborn, though, which often drove me to do the opposite of what was expected of me. I wanted to find out more about Franz's life. I wanted him to tell me about his country, his ambitions and his plans. I also needed to believe in the goodness of the world. "Come what may," I said to myself.

So I asked him my first question, the one that had preyed on my mind from the start: "Why me?"

He stood gaping at me for a few seconds and then whispered, "What did you say?"

"Why did you choose me to chat with? There are so many people here you could have talked to. You told me, the first time, that you had been observing me for a few days. What makes me so different from the others?"

He hesitated for a few more seconds before answering. I wondered if he really trusted me, because I, too, could very well have denounced him to earn a few favours from the senior officers.

He gently explained that he had noticed right away how I looked the soldiers in the eye when they gave me an order.

My candid gaze had impressed him greatly. He mentioned my posture, always straight, never that of a victim, and added that I radiated a strength that, to him, bordered on provocation.

He also said he found me interesting and wanted me to have a good opinion of him. He stressed he wasn't a torturer nor a heartless person, that he was human, with weaknesses and feelings.

"I'm not the least bit interested in this conflict," he admitted. "Before it began, my only wish was to be a journalist and travel the world. Since the war broke out, I have thanked God every day for not being forced to carry out cruel orders. I managed to get out of it by doing a lot of translation and administrative work. I know, though, that very soon I'll be sent to the front because we have lost far more soldiers than expected."

He suddenly fell silent and resumed his patrol to make sure no one had seen or heard him speaking to me. I needed a few moments to recover from what he just said about me. I wasn't expecting so much interest and so many compliments from someone I was supposed to hate with a vengeance. Was he being honest? I sensed he was sincere and meant what he said.

At the same time, I wondered why I felt so excited whenever I saw him and he spoke to me, why my heart began to beat faster. Although I was choked with emotion and wanted to cry, I had to control myself so as not to attract attention. The comparison might seem far-fetched, but I felt like a child in an orphanage that had just been chosen and instantly fell in love with its new parents. Who could tell me what was happening within me? I couldn't confide in anyone and that added to my confusion.

I was about to ask him another question when we heard quick footsteps on the large staircase. Two soldiers came to get a woman. We never saw her again, of course. She was French. No doubt she was a member of the Resistance and they wanted to make her talk. That happened often. Later, in the evening, Mathilde would confirm my fears. That woman was the wife of a very active Resistance fighter and she had often mentioned her husband's exploits to her bedmates.

When the midday siren sounded, Franz's shift ended. We stole glances at each other that seemed to say, "What a pity. See you soon perhaps!"

The rest of the day flew by. I floated through it as though on a cloud. This new friendship was changing me. I observed the women around me, thin, without hair, gaunt faces, and realized I must look just like them. I tried to understand why Franz took an interest in me while I had never been as ugly in all my life. Did he have something at the back of his mind, something he meant to ask me? What did I have to offer him?

In the end I convinced myself that our conversations were purely of a friendly nature, since, for my part, I didn't have a single attribute resembling those of a woman at that time. But can friendship cause so much inner turmoil? I felt like talking it over with Simone and having her explain what was happening inside me, except I was afraid of her anger. It was still too early to share my secret, or too late. My mind was in a muddle.

In the evening, when I returned to our mattress, I noticed that Iréna was more feverish than the day before. The previous night, she had snuggled up closer against my back than usual because she was shivering. Her temperature hadn't dropped; I had no idea how she had even managed to finish her day's work. Half an hour after the evening ration, which she hadn't been able to get down, her temperature was so high she became delirious. Simone was beside herself. She asked me what we should do, but I didn't know.

Although Mathilde hadn't come back from her shift yet, we decided to take Iréna to the infirmary even though we had sworn to each other we would never take a decision without the consent of all four of us. We really had no choice because we didn't know where Mathilde was.

I went to get the soldier on guard duty and motioned him to follow me. He looked at Iréna, without touching her of course, and came back with two soldiers in charge of the infirmary. Simone and I helped them to put her on the stretcher and they carried her away. When we lifted her up, we noticed that she was very thin and fragile. We both wondered if she was going to pull through. We cried a lot. I prayed as hard as I could, while realizing at the same time that I had been praying less and less.

When Mathilde returned, we told her what had happened. She got angry. She reminded us we did take an oath. She had good reason to believe that Iréna would never come back to us, especially if at the infirmary they discovered the tattoo on her arm. We tried to reassure her. With such a fever, we told her, no one would dare touch her because they would be afraid she might be infectious.

Mathilde went on criticizing us for our decision. She could have done something, she said. Yet Simone and I had tried everything to help our friend and didn't see what more we could have done. We asked Mathilde how she would have acted in our place and she snapped back that she would have been able to find medication. To prove her point, she pulled out a small package wrapped in a towel, which she had hidden under her dress, and threw it on the mattress. The package contained a sausage to be shared at bedtime. Simone hurriedly covered it up so no one would see it and ordered Mathilde to calm down.

"I don't wish to know where you got that meat," she told her. "I'll wait until you are ready to explain where you have been when you come back late. For now, you have no right to blame us for making a decision without you. You weren't here and we were worried. I don't want Armande and me to be punished because you are shouting at the top of your voice. Will you change your tone, please?"

Mathilde calmed down. She knew Simone was justified in speaking to her like this. Quietly she began to tell us that thanks to her accountant's job, she was in contact with two officers who could grant her some privileges. They considered she was doing good work; the inventories had never been as accurate nor the accounts clearer. They often checked the books and hadn't found a single mistake. This sausage was the first present they had given her. We asked no more questions.

I would have liked to tell them what had happened to me today with Franz. With their experience, they could have explained and analyzed what I felt for him. But I thought it better to keep my secret. I didn't want them to lecture me. We were worried enough about Iréna's fate and began to dream up plans to gain access to the infirmary.

As soon as the lights were switched off, we divided up the sausage and ate it in silence. We thanked Mathilde from the bottom of our hearts for this present. She must have gone to a great deal of trouble for it. Naturally we hid Iréna's piece in our mattress.

❖ ❖ ❖

The following day, we had barely opened our eyes when an officer brought us another girl to share our mattress with. Did this mean that Iréna had died of her fever? We didn't know. In the meantime we had to split our bowl of brown liquid with this stranger. No one wanted to discriminate. We were all in the same hell, and our strength lay in supporting each other. We all realized that. But it was difficult nonetheless to accept another prisoner taking the place of the one who had become our friend and whose life we wanted to save. Iréna had become a symbol. She was the one motivating us in our struggle to survive, the one we defended, at our own risk. For all these reasons we just couldn't be friendly with the newcomer.

But there was hardly any time to talk to her. We had to start our daily routine. Simone and Mathilde would both try to find out more about Iréna's condition. I naturally worried about Iréna and didn't like that she had been replaced like this. But even so, all I could think of was Franz.

I settled myself at my machine and saw Franz coming up to me. I began to shake. He seemed really happy to see me and smiled broadly. He wanted to know how I was.

"I can tell you, Franz, that apart from our conversations, which do me a lot of good, everything depresses me. Most of all, I wonder how I'll find the strength to hold on until the end. I don't know anything about this war. I don't even know exactly why I was arrested. Could you tell me a little more about it? Will it be much longer? How much more time will we be spending here, in these degrading conditions?"

Then I had the audacity to mention his leader. "Everyone says Hitler is mad." I realized I had just made a very risky remark. How could I be sure Franz wouldn't turn against me? Also, someone might have heard me …

I glanced around. Everything seemed normal. Franz looked around, too. Then he answered, speaking faster than usual:

"Many Germans, myself included, think he is very danger-ous. In 1928 he already stated in one of his speeches that in a struggle for life the strongest, the fittest won, while the least able, the weaker one lost. Hitler leads his party in accordance with an incorrect interpretation of the work of Charles Darwin and his theory of natural selection. This helps us to understand the ideology of Nazism, which considers man to be an animal with animal values. The brute who wins has to win if he is the stronger one. The child that dies has to die if it is the weakest."

I was fascinated by what he told me. I began to make more sense of Hitler's thinking, although I grasped by no means all the aspects of Nazi theory.

Franz checked his watch. His spell of duty was nearly finished. He turned to me, looking sad. That touched me. I had no experience of life but was intelligent enough to understand that from now on what I called for the time being a friendly connection wouldn't be exactly restful.

The Injury

When I woke up the following morning, I asked Simone how she thought I looked. My question puzzled her. "Why do you want to know? I hope you haven't talked to that soldier?" I replied half a second too late. Simone had guessed. She cradled her head in her hands. "Oh, no! It isn't true! I don't believe it!"

I promised I would deal with this relationship on my own and to tell her everything so long as she didn't criticize me. She opened her mouth, but nothing came out. At last she told me that my face hadn't got too thin, my cheeks weren't too hollow, and I still had a little doll's face. I kissed her on the cheek and went off to work.

He was already there! I was afraid he might notice how excited I was, so I tried to look relaxed. He asked me if I wanted to continue yesterday's conversation.

I nodded in agreement while carrying on with my work. Before he began to speak, I asked him very quickly and without raising my voice what the reason was for this hatred and hounding of the Jews. Franz replied that unfortunately the persecution of the Jewish people went back a long way. The Jews had been the victims of prejudices for centuries and were even prohibited from holding certain jobs and entering some professions.

"Not too long ago, Jews couldn't own land nor farm it," Franz told me. "After the First World War, anti-Semitism was commonplace in Germany. The existence of extermination camps was confirmed only recently. When people told us about such horrors, we didn't want to believe them. At first there was denial, but later we had to admit they existed. Then shame took hold. People kept quiet and pretended it wasn't true. The first of these camps, Dachau, opened its gates in the early 1930s. When they were released, prisoners had to sign a document in which they committed themselves never to talk about what they had experienced there, under penalty of being automatically sent back to the camp. There were many Germans who believed or chose to believe that the concentration camps were "merely" places where enemies of the Nazi party were punished. They also thought the reign of terror only applied to political opponents and Jews. They regarded this as normal.

Suddenly Franz fell silent. We had almost been caught. We needed to be even more vigilant.

Whenever he stopped talking to me and looking at me, I felt lonely right away. And when we had to end a conversation, I realized how hard it would it be for me to go on enduring this horror if I never saw him again. When he left, I concentrated on my work. I looked down so no one would see me cry.

❖ ❖ ❖

Four days went by without him showing himself. I obviously couldn't ask his replacement what had happened to him, although I wanted to very badly.

When I saw him again, on the fifth day, my excitement reached fever pitch and I found it difficult to quiet down. I was wondering if he had any idea how I felt when he was away. But I could see from the look he flashed at me that he'd understood.

He explained, as though to apologize, that he was assigned to different tasks every day and never knew where he would be sent next. That's why he couldn't let me know beforehand. This calmed me down. I decided to make the most of each minute; never mind how much time we still had together or the void our parting would inevitably leave.

Franz asked me once again if I would like him to pick up the conversation from where we left off. I nodded. I even reminded him that when he'd had to leave, he was just trying to explain why the Germans hounded and despised the Jewish people.

Franz then described to me in detail how the roundups of Jews were conducted. Soldiers had been specially trained to hunt them down, in the utmost secrecy. He told me that 80 percent of the denunciations were done by private citizens. I couldn't believe it! But most surprising of all was that the police or the Gestapo didn't even reward those who handed over Jews. They were ordinary citizens, not even members of the Nazi Party. The Jews distinguished themselves by their way of living, which was different from that of the majority of Germans. People who cracked a joke about Hitler were likely to be betrayed, too. Denunciations could also result from self-interest. Someone would want to take over the apartment of a Jewish family, so then that person denounced the family. Someone might find his neighbours too much of a nuisance, same thing.

"I heard another story, which is just as appalling," he went on. "The Jewish neighbour of a family member of mine was driven with other Jews from Nuremberg to a stadium where the grass was particularly long. To humiliate them and show them they were truly at the bottom of the ladder, soldiers forced them to cut the grass with their teeth, or graze on it, no more no less. Do you really think, Armande, that I can agree with that?"

I began to cry, looking down at my machine.

Franz continued, "If a bullet could put an end to my life, I wouldn't have to be ashamed of being German anymore, later on, when the war is over. How will I be able to live after this conflict? It will be impossible to pretend none of this ever existed. That's why I would like to live somewhere else, not out of denial, but so I wouldn't have to look every day at the images and places of this slaughter, which has dishonoured every German."

Franz's spell of duty was now finished. He told me he would be working in the administrative services for the next two weeks. He assured me he would ask to be sent back here as soon as his assignment had been completed.

The following night I tossed about restlessly in my sleep. Franz was now part of my dreams. In one of these dreams I walked along with him in Paris, clinging to his arm. I was elegantly dressed, like those women he described, whom he used to meet during his strolls on the Champs-Elysées. My hair had grown long and was drawn back into a chignon. I wore a small hat on top of my head, with a veil that fell over my nose. We really looked like a pair of lovers. We chatted and laughed a lot. It was a sunny day. I often dreamed of sun-filled days while I was in captivity, and would always be disappointed when I woke up. How is it possible to spend so many years without seeing daylight?

Dreams were essential to us. They were our only means of escape. Iréna told us for example that her dreams about her mother's food satisfied her hunger.

I had another dream, a much less enjoyable one. Franz and I were caught in the middle of a conversation. Officers took Franz away, and I never saw him again. All this was likely to happen, but I hoped it would be as late as possible. I prayed to God that He answer my prayers. I continued to keep my feelings for Franz to myself, wanting to preserve my relationship with my other friends.

I began to count backwards the days before Franz's return. My first working day without contact with him was surely the longest I had lived through since I arrived at the camp and since we met.

Did *he* think about our conversations now and then? Was I in love with my torturer or was it just friendship? In the end I wondered if everything hadn't been easier for me before I met Franz.

The days came and went and my mind was still just as full of Franz. I was tired of thinking about him all the time. I went through the whole gamut of emotions. It was naive of me to believe in him, I thought, foolish to be so romantic. Weren't this man and my values poles apart? I felt guilty for falling into the trap of the girl who is excited by a sudden interest from a man.

One evening Simone reported to us that she had spoken to a prisoner who worked with her in the kitchens. This woman had the job of taking meals to the sick in the infirmary. She had seen Iréna and gave Simone a description of her condition. Iréna's temperature hadn't really dropped. She had dysentery and was completely dehydrated. We were very worried about her.

We had to find a way to come to her aid at any cost, but it wasn't easy. Mathilde obtained permission to make a lightning visit to the infirmary. She particularly wanted to make sure the tattooed number on Iréna's arm was still covered up. If not, she was ready to take care of it.

She told us that as a result of the typhus epidemic that was spreading throughout the camp the infirmary was crammed full. Iréna remained almost incognito in all that commotion. It was vitally important to ensure she wouldn't be sent somewhere else or be killed. Mathilde had overheard a conversation among the officers. They had said that the SS no longer hesitated to eliminate the sick and the weak. These prisoners were killed by phenol injections because the SS needed to make room in the infirmary. It was like euthanizing a sick animal. They also tried out various vaccines on patients. To do this, they would leave some typhus sufferers untreated. These patients were called "transmitters." They served to keep the virus alive and at the disposal of the SS doctors, who used the transmitters' blood to infect other prisoners.

Mathilde got in touch with an inmate of French birth who worked in the infirmary, and promised to regularly bring her a few extra food rations in exchange for which her caring for Iréna had to take precedence over that of other patients. She should definitely not report the tattooed number on her skin. This Frenchwoman could apparently be trusted.

Meanwhile, we got to know the woman who had taken Iréna's place on our mattress a little better. She was called Karina and was a Romany.

I had never heard that word before. After a few days, or, to be more truthful, as soon as we were sure we could trust her, we asked her a number of questions about her people. We learnt that the Romanies have a common Indian origin. They were also called Gypsies, Manush, Roma, Tziganes, or Romanichals. Since people considered them to be of tainted stock, they began to travel all over the world, no doubt to escape from society's rejection.

Several years after the war, I found out that the Romanies, this nomadic people of no fixed abode who travelled in caravans from town to town, village to village, had been the subject of a genocide that went almost unnoticed. Historians have estimated there were 250,000 to 500,000 victims out of a population of 700,000 Romanies in Europe. They suffered virtually the same fate as the Jews. For a long time this tragedy was hushed up, as if it hadn't happened.

Karine was twenty-four and had jet-black eyes lined with very thick lashes. Before her hair, which I imagined had been as black as her eyes, was shaved off, she must have been a great beauty. Quite small but sturdy; there was nothing frail about her.

During a selection process following her arrest, she had been examined like a cart horse, and the officials concluded she would be perfect for heavy work. That's how she ended up at the Buchenwald camp. Her job was demanding; she packed up the arms we produced and carried boxes from one place to another all day.

As I watched her, I noticed she wasn't afraid of anything. She greedily ate her food portions, and it seemed to me she was immune to every illness. The difficult living conditions of her people must have given her the strength to survive the horror.

She stayed with us as long as Iréna's illness lasted. For a long time, that is. While Iréna was treated for dysentery, she developed a lump in her neck, which was so large that the doctor in charge decided to remove it. But sanitary conditions weren't the best. And what was bound to happen happened. The wound became infected; pus oozed out of it. The prisoners who worked in the infirmary unfortunately wiped it away with dirty cloths. At last, after three weeks, Mathilde managed — God knows how — to find sulfa drugs.

While Franz was still away, the machine I worked with broke down. I had no idea what had happened. I examined it closely, but didn't spot anything unusual.

I immediately alerted the guard who paced up and down in front of me, but he walked on without looking in my direction. So I started shouting as loud as I could, "Hey! I can't work anymore! It won't run!"

When I saw that he kept on walking, ignoring me completely, I stuck my tongue out at him. He flew into a rage and hit me on the front of my leg with the bayonet of his rifle. Then he resumed his pacing as if nothing had happened.

I had a cut of about seven or eight inches, and the wound bled profusely. I didn't have any clean cloths to stem the blood and therefore used my dress to mop up as much of it as I could and stop the bleeding.

I cried with pain, but even more with rage. I struggled to sit down again and, keeping my head lowered so the guard wouldn't see my tears, tried to pull myself together. I cannot say how much time passed before the whistle announced the end of the work day. I mustered up my courage and dragged myself to the counting room. When the girls saw what state I was in, they rushed forward to help and support me. I nearly fainted, but they kept tight hold of me. That way I was able to remain standing during roll call.

While the officers bustled about doing something else, Simone applied a tourniquet to my leg with my bootlace. The blood stopped flowing. She advised me not to take off my boot because it would be impossible to put it on again. She was right. The swelling was already quite advanced. I stayed upright for two hours, in great pain.

Mathilde lined up afterwards for my evening ration. My pain was greater than my appetite, but Simone recommended that I eat to keep up my strength.

Immediately after curfew, I gave my dress to Simone, who hid it under hers and asked permission to go to the toilets, where she tried to wash the blood out of my dress with the thin trickle of water from the tap.

The cloth used for wrapping the chunk of sausage we were keeping for Iréna protected my wound during the night and the following two days. Mathilde stole two pieces of fabric from a first-aid kit in the administrative offices.

Simone did everything she could to help me, and her support was a great comfort. When she attended to my wound, it wasn't just out of solidarity; to me, it looked like the love of a mother who wants to save her child at any cost. She did it without asking *the* question, which, I knew, she longed to pose: "Do you still want to put your trust in a soldier?" I very much appreciated her silence.

The day after this savage attack, the machine had been repaired. I was relieved to see yesterday's soldier was not on duty. I certainly couldn't have helped staring at him with the fury of a wounded animal. I knew I would have exploded if he'd looked at me with condescension and I definitely wouldn't be here today writing down my story.

The incident had dealt my morale a severe blow. I now had doubts about Franz's goodness. I questioned my talks with him. I had shown open-mindedness toward the enemy, but it hadn't served me well. Although I missed Franz, I didn't look forward to his return quite as eagerly. If I ever spoke to him again, I would be much less pleasant. My pride had been affected just as much as my leg. I didn't want Franz to look upon me as an injured victim who couldn't retaliate. I was obviously down in the dumps and needed to get a grip on myself. My anger helped me nonetheless to forget about my leg somewhat. When the siren announced the end of that first work day after the accident, it came as a relief, although it took an enormous effort to walk to the attendance room.

After a few days, my wound healed on the surface, but a yellow liquid dripped from the cut's centre. A red patch appeared around the swelling. Obviously, infection had set in.

One morning, Simone came back with a piece of bread soaked in milk, stolen from the kitchens. She cut the bread into small bits and applied these to the red spots. Then she tightened the dressing around the wound. I had once seen my grandmother prepare such a poultice to treat a sore that was slow to heal. I limped to my work station.

The milk and the bread seemed to have an effect because I began to have sharp pains in the wound. I needed to use my injured leg all day to press down on the pedal activating the pin that fastened the bullet. Whenever the injury sent me a pain signal, I relived the scene in spite of myself and felt rage surge through me.

When Simone changed my dressing that evening, we noticed a distinct improvement, no doubt because of the milk-soaked bread. The wound wasn't nearly as red, but there was still a bit of yellowish liquid inside it. All along, I was grateful to Simone for applying a tourniquet with my bootlace on the day of the accident; without her intervention, I would certainly have bled to death. We were living in hellish conditions, but luckily we had forged strong bonds of friendship and that encouraged us to surpass ourselves in helping others. I had never had the opportunity to know and experience such compassion, not even during my life as a nun.

At last, we received news of Iréna. Her wound infection had subsided, but her diarrhea started again, and she was far too weak to leave the infirmary. To make matters worse, she had broken her nose when she fell off a stretcher on her way to the toilets. We couldn't take any more bad news. It affected our spirits as well as our physical health.

Even though my leg hurt, I was relieved I didn't have a temperature. Gangrene was liable to set in if the wound wasn't treated properly. Simone and I always examined it carefully so we could react without delay if it turned black or began to give off a foul smell. Fortunately Mathilde managed to find sulfa drugs, as she had for Iréna, and they unquestionably saved my leg.

Simone knew that Mathilde granted sexual favours to the soldiers in order to get all these privileges, but she didn't suspect the half of what the soldiers asked of her for every favour granted. And I, I didn't really know what "to provide sex" meant. It was all quite abstract to me.

Simone had got married late in life to Léon. So she had experienced some sexual freedom and was much more aware of the price Mathilde needed to pay to get these privileges for us. As for me, who had difficulty understanding what went on inside me when I happened to be with Franz, one can imagine how naive I was on the subject. I only found out much later what Mathilde endured for us, but I won't talk about it because I wouldn't want to tarnish, by giving certain sordid details, the memory of a woman who would have deserved more medals than a number of highly placed officers, for all the lives she saved.

I will never forget what she had to put up with to protect us from death. Every little favour we benefited from carried a steep price to be paid to the soldiers. Even her visits to Iréna in the infirmary, lasting barely five minutes, needed to be paid back. Our requirements for drugs, Iréna's and mine, were so glaring that she didn't hesitate to provoke the soldiers so she could get some.

I can imagine the kind of deal she had to make to prevent our three names and hers from coming up in the Lottery of Death. She would never give us details about the pact she had entered into with the soldiers. But I have always wondered how she was able to suffer the utmost humiliation and agree to be touched without desiring it, and even having to pretend she enjoyed it, no doubt. When the time came to thank her, she merely said, "You would have done the same thing in my place. It's a matter of survival." I honestly think I would have been much more of a coward.

My leg was getting better by the day and I limped less and less. In spite of the yellow liquid that hadn't stopped leaking from the wound, there was no infection.

I still felt just as angry with the soldier who had hurt me, but after much thought, I couldn't blame Franz. Quite the opposite. If there was a balm to be put on my injury and on this whole dreadful life, the talks with Franz might be part of it.

Franz had said he would be back in two weeks. To count the days, I put one machine-gun bullet aside, in my workbox, after each day.

At last Iréna came back to us and Karina was transferred. Mathilde reassured us by saying she wasn't too worried for now about Karina's fate because she was a very good worker. She never slowed her pace and had an extraordinary amount of energy. As long as that didn't change, she wouldn't need to fear for her life. We had avoided becoming too attached to her, since we knew she would leave as soon as Iréna returned. Once again Mathilde had "seen to it" that Iréna, upon leaving the infirmary, rejoined the three of us. When she arrived on our mattress, she was still weak, but had to show up for work the next day without fail, or else …

Iréna gave us news of Krystina, of whom we had caught brief glimpses since she gave birth. She no longer spoke and looked straight ahead, like a robot. Iréna told us her little Inga had lived only three weeks because her mother didn't have enough milk. Although she had grown weaker, she had been forced to go back to work very soon after the delivery. During the breaks, she tried to feed her daughter, but she had no more milk. The women who worked at the infirmary made attempts to feed her with milk that was more like water than anything else, but it was no good, and Inga died a few days later. Then Krystina went back to the infirmary, suffering from severe depression. She was never seen again. As we listened to this story, we cried bitterly. Once again our morale took a blow. No one could say when this hell would end.

We went to sleep curled up against one another as never before. We wanted to celebrate Iréna's return, having missed her so much, and we needed to warm ourselves, body and soul. It seemed to me that in all the time we had shared a mattress, our bodies had never been so attuned to each other. Every night, we went to sleep in the spoon position. We were the four pieces of a single set of cutlery.

Farewell to Franz

I carefully recounted the bullets I'd put in my workbox. I hadn't made a mistake: Franz was expected back tomorrow. The thought of seeing him again excited me. I'd struggled to calm down for the past two days. My sudden good mood might be offensive to many, given the situation and the place we were in.

I was so filled with my new-found happiness that I lost my appetite. I burst with energy such as I hadn't experienced for a long time. I even made the girls laugh by imitating a Quebecker from the Saguenay–Lac-Saint-Jean area who tries to speak German. I'd never seen Mathilde in that state; her giggles lasted until curfew. She had dropped all her defences. *I* felt more like crying. We had a good time once again. Laughter was like tears: when you suppressed it for too long, you couldn't stop it once you gave in to it. And that was all to the good.

When we woke up, Mathilde rubbed the top of my head. "You're completely mad!" she said, remembering the previous night's laughing fits. I was really proud to have cheered her up.

I had slept very little, but felt wonderful nevertheless. Before seeing Franz again, I would have liked to look at myself in a mirror, comb my hair, put on lipstick, but none of that was possible. Still, I could smile, I thought. And I did, discreetly of course, as I walked toward the staple machine.

Franz was already there. I smiled at him. Instead of looking at me, he stared right away at my injured leg. Then he came toward me, forgetting we each had our own role. He immediately checked himself. I sat down on my work chair. He took several steps, breathed deeply, as though to try and calm down, and asked me if the wound was healing well. I reassured him and admitted I had somewhat provoked the soldier who injured me.

He muttered between his teeth that he couldn't even ask me who had done this because, if he gave him a good thrashing, it would instantly backfire on me. He was terribly sorry.

Surprised he wanted to protect me, I didn't know what to say. He obviously cared for me and didn't want anything bad to happen to me. I was deeply moved. I suddenly felt important in his eyes. I couldn't hold back my tears, couldn't speak. I wanted to tell him I was happy to see him and my life stopped when I couldn't talk to him, but I just went on crying.

He fell silent. I didn't even hear him breathe anymore. I raised my head and saw him looking shaken. He didn't say a word. Did he feel the way I did? I wanted to think so. I had quieted down and was able to admit to him that since the day of that injury I no longer trusted him quite as much.

I had something to ask him, a question that tormented me, and I wanted a straight answer. "Franz, if you ever receive the order to perform the Lottery of Death when you are on guard duty, how are going to get out of it?"

He was dumbstruck. The possibility had never occurred to him. He replied candidly, "You know, the first thought that comes to my mind … is to pretend I feel ill, while I writhe with pain, because I don't have the right to disobey orders. You make me shake with fear, Armande. Until now, I have never had to kill or mistreat anyone. I have mainly had administrative jobs to do. But the war is becoming more and more difficult for the German army, and I know I'll soon be required to carry out orders I won't agree with. I would rather fight at the front. I know they'll need me before long. Do I have to tell you I am very frightened? Yet don't feel embarrassed about that. I sometimes wonder how I'd be able to live if I ever felt the urge to desert. I'm sure I would be tormented by shame for having forsaken my country. Because of my father and my upbringing. I wouldn't be able to look my family in the face anymore."

For three days we felt an urgent need to go on talking and forge an even closer bond. To encourage him to come and visit me, I tried to give him a taste for my country by describing the wide-open spaces, the four clearly distinct seasons, the great distances between towns. Paris might be a unique, extraordinary city, but nonetheless he had to see Quebec one day. I told him that the warm-hearted people of my region would make him very welcome.

To Franz, Quebec and Austria seemed to have much in common.

I abruptly stopped talking. Where exactly could he come to visit me? At the convent? I had forgotten who I was. That cruel reality made my stomach churn. When I got out of here, I would have to enter another prison. It would be impossible to stroll about freely with Franz. I was young and inexperienced, and in my imagination I pictured an ideal world where everything would be easy.

If I came out of this war alive, would I still hear the call of God? I wondered. Was I really made for that life? Did I have enough faith to be happy? After experiencing so many hardships, why wouldn't I choose to be free? And if I did, how would I overcome the disgrace of renouncing my vows?

No doubt about it: My bond with Franz was upsetting all the plans made for me. What did I expect from him? That he would join me in Quebec, whose natural wonders I had just praised? But that would mean I would no longer be a nun when I returned.… And if Franz ever arrived in Quebec, what kind of a couple would we make? Would we be that couple who had come together in turmoil, who had met in an enclosed place marked by horror? How would we cope with the judgment of others?

However that might be, he told me on the fourth day what I didn't want to hear: he had to leave for the front the next morning.

I expected the worst. Everything would fall apart for me after he left. What was the use of trying to make it through in those conditions?

Franz arranged to meet me in Paris, at the café at the Louvre, on the first May 7 after the war. This was the date of our first conversation at the camp.

"I will understand perfectly if you don't come, because our two lives are so very different. It was a real pleasure to talk to you. It's a pity, I think, that we met during this awful war. I wish you good luck and keep on being a fighter. It's the only way to survive."

Survive? How would I? Since I started talking to him, Franz had become my inspiration to carry on, my sole reason for resisting. Thanks to him, I could forget the suffering and the hell I was in.

Over the following days, I was inconsolable. My friends tried to talk to me, in vain because I had withdrawn into myself. Then, bit by bit, the grief subsided.

All wasn't easy in the beginning, of course, and I often tossed about in my sleep. Sometimes gloom swept over me. One morning I got up determined to come out of the camp alive. From then on, that thought was my only reason to live.

In the end, Franz became my happiest memory of those dark years. Thank you, Franz!

Liberation

The last two years of imprisonment were particularly harsh. We had turned into zombies. We walked because we had to and we ate because we had to. It was as though we no longer existed, as though we had become empty shells. We had grown insensitive to all those girls dying around us of malnutrition, exhaustion, or simply despair, and this was unacceptable.

In fact, Mathilde kept telling us we mustn't let ourselves go. Every night, she spurred us on. "Really, we haven't survived all this to die now! Pull yourselves together, girls. I know it's difficult, but we have to get out of here alive."

She often held Iréna up as an example, who would surely have died a long time ago if she hadn't been with us. "Don't tell me you don't want to see the day we put our noses outside, proud we have stood up to the devil!"

Of course we wanted that. No one wanted to die. The problem is when there's not even a shred of hope left and we wonder what use it is to keep standing. At that point, death no longer scares us.

But Mathilde always managed to keep the faint glimmer alive. "Haven't you noticed that the soldiers on guard are older all the time? It means the Germans have lost a lot of men in action and Germany will very likely lose the war. Don't give up hope. It will soon be over."

It was true. All the soldiers we had been familiar with until quite recently were gone. Throughout these two years, the memory of Franz helped me to stay alive. As soon as I could, I would take refuge in my memories. I had created an imaginary world around him. I would picture pleasant scenes in which he was always there, beside me. My imagination knew no bounds. At night, I saw the film of our life projected on the ceiling of the room. We had first got married in his village and naturally I had made my wedding dress myself. We travelled a lot after that, back and forth between our two countries. Then Franz decided to settle in Quebec with me. Our house wasn't large. It was white and stood at the foot of a mountain, so he would feel more at home. We were very much in love. Quietly, as the months went by, I entered the bedroom with him. It wasn't so simple at first. I was ill at ease on our wedding night. But Franz hugged me very tightly, and, with infinite tact and gentleness, took off my clothes piece by piece.

His kisses were delicious. He kissed my neck and I shivered all over. Little by little, I began to caress him, too. The caresses I imagined I would give him, lasting for hours, centered for the most part on his chest, his back and his neck. Of his anatomy from his waist to his knees, I had no idea. No one had ever told me anything. Nothing either on what happened next between a man and a woman. These wonderful secret thoughts of my imaginary life with Franz helped me to get through the real nightmare I was living.

❖ ❖ ❖

The last year of our detention seemed like an eternity. Sometimes, the mood inside the camp changed completely and it almost looked as if the nightmare would soon be over. There were only about a hundred survivors left in our building, and production in the factory often broke down. The soldiers who now guarded us were veterans of the war of 1914–18.

Even so, we thought it would never end. The last six months were longer than the past three and a half years. We had begun to defy the authorities because we were less and less afraid. Sitting on our mattresses, we would spend entire days chatting instead of going to work. The straw had never been changed since our arrival, and the stench was unbearable, but our sense of smell seemed to be numbed. Bad smells were everywhere and we had probably got used to them.

For the hundred or so remaining girls, there were now only three guards. One day, one of them kicked a girl because she wouldn't get up. She couldn't take it anymore and wanted to die. We all began to stamp our feet and thump our fists in our hands while moving toward them, and they backed away. We were very proud to have confronted them and shown them that from now on we refused to accept the unacceptable. We were becoming human beings again.

For hours on end we talked about what we would do after our release, if ever we were lucky enough to make it through. Simone wanted to be reunited with her Léon, of course. She vowed that if she got her old life back she would never complain again and would always be content with her lot. She promised above all to commit the sins of the flesh and gluttony as often as possible. "And if I don't go to heaven, who cares!" she concluded.

Mathilde also wanted to go back to the life she had before her arrest. She meant to savour everything, like Simone, to revive her sense of smell with heady scents, become an elegant woman again, with exquisite clothes, and find a man, only one, with whom she would share the rest of her life.

Iréna's only wish was to get out of this hell alive. Because of the number tattooed on her skin, she would always remember what she had gone through in these long years of confinement. She wanted to return to Poland, to meet up with her mother and sister again, and make sure they were in good health. At the same time, she said she was very much afraid of what she would discover.

And I, Armande, what did I want? The first thing that came into my mind was to take a bath. As for the rest of my life, I was utterly confused. I felt less of a desire to be a nun. After all those deprivations, I badly wanted to be free, in every way.

Our wishes would be granted …

❀ ❀ ❀

For the past three days, we had been left on our own, without any guards. The food had run out and we didn't know what to do. But if we didn't take action, we would certainly die in this vile hole.

Mathilde and another strong girl in the camp tried to convince us that we had to go up the stairs to the exit, to see what was happening. Not everyone agreed, for sure. Some said the war might be over, which explained why there were no soldiers around. Others thought the soldiers would be back in a minute and if we made any kind of move, we could count on serious reprisals. Several of us, including me, believed it was a trap and once we were up there, we would all be shot.

Mathilde remained convinced we needed to act quickly and she had a strong argument: if we stayed here, we were all going to die anyway. No doubt she was right.

Then she worked out a plan. We were going to hold hands and hug the wall as we went up the steps in single file. When we saw daylight, we would put up our hands so they wouldn't fire at us. Mathilde would lead the way, and the other girl who vigorously supported her plan would bring up the rear.

I never trembled as violently in my whole life. I hung on to Simone's hand like a child who didn't want to go outside. And Simone drew me up. There were about a hundred steps, and it seemed to me as though the climbing would never end. Some girls were so scared they urinated on the spot, and most of them prayed aloud. I prayed to God and the Virgin Mary with a powerful voice I didn't know I had. The prayers I recited before that day were nothing like these!

When we saw a glimmer of daylight appear, we did exactly what Mathilde had asked us to do. Blinded by the light, we raised our arms skyward, as high as possible, to be sure we would be seen. The farther we climbed, the brighter the light. We had trouble keeping our eyes open as it was extremely painful. When my foot landed on the top step, I had my eyes closed because of the glare. At last I felt the wind on my skin, my lungs filled with fresh air, and I heard an infernal din coming from above.

I thought the Germans were arriving to kill us. I looked up towards the noise and saw helicopters. I had never seen these flying objects before. Underneath the helicopters, we could see a red cross.

One of the girls shouted, "We're saved! The Red Cross is here!" When I heard that shout and I knew someone else was taking charge of my life, my body became extremely heavy. It was as though every part of it, having endured too much, began to cry out its pain. I had held on until then, but now I let myself go. I was completely worn out. I just had time to think this was the best day of my life before I fainted.

It was April 11, 1945.

❖ ❖ ❖

I woke up in a hospital in Paris. I heard we had travelled here by train, but not in cattle cars this time. I made the trip on a stretcher.

The hospital room was huge. There were about twenty of us, in small metal beds, as at the convent. The first thing that struck me was how white and clean the place was. At the three camps where I'd lived for more than four years, I had only seen the colour grey and utter filth. The first movement I made after regaining consciousness was to sniff the sheets. I instantly recognized the smell of the laundry and began to cry. When I noticed the contrast between the white sheet and the black colour of my skin, I cried even more.

To make my skin white again and especially to get rid of the dirt that had become embedded in it over the past four years, nurses would give me sulphur baths every day for close to a year. Despite its rotten-egg odour, sulphur removes grime and stops the spread of infectious diseases.

The first baths I took smelled awful. I couldn't bear it and fainted several times. It took months before the beneficial effects became visible. We were also entitled to baths without sulphur. These were sheer delights.

On the first day, I looked for my three friends with whom I'd shared a mattress, but only Simone was in the room with me. I found out that Mathilde and Iréna had been placed elsewhere. I was glad to see Simone again. The nurses told me she had remained conscious on the journey back and always close to me. She protected me to the end. That's why the hospital staff had put her in a bed beside me.

Now it was my turn to watch her sleep and rest, and a feeling of pure happiness engulfed me. She slept for nearly a week, just like me. I would fall asleep at any time of the day. The first mornings, the nurses often found us lying on the floor under a blanket. We had to gradually get used to the comfort of a bed again. We also needed to relearn to eat normally. We had to start with small doses, with clear broth and warm milk. Many prisoners died when they were freed because they had been given too much food too quickly. Their stomachs couldn't take it.

At the time of my arrest, my weight was a hundred and eighteen pounds. When the nurses weighed me, it was eighty-five pounds. I had lost thirty-three pounds. I wanted to see myself in a mirror. I got a big surprise: Not only did I no longer recognize myself, but it looked as though my eyes had moved towards the back of my skull. My image scared me. The nurses did their best to reassure me: In a few months, my face would become the way it was.

Gradually my appetite returned. I was anxious to be my old self again. Still, after surviving so many deprivations, I didn't want to die from eating too much. I also asked myself many questions about my future, but for now I chose to rest. Yet I needed to deal with reality sooner than expected. A few days after our hospitalization, the staff had to identify us, by asking for our name and where we lived before the war. We also had to tell them whom they should contact to let them know we were still alive.

So the congregation was notified of my being at the Lutetia hotel, which had been temporarily turned into a hospital to accommodate the overflow of sick people. A few weeks later, a nun from my community in Brittany paid me a visit. When I saw her, I remained unmoved, totally indifferent. Probably because I didn't know her very well. To be honest, I didn't want us to discuss my faith.

The visit chilled me even further when the nun informed me that the community required a thorough medical checkup and had to make sure I was still a virgin before it welcomed me back in its house. When she had gone, I became myself again, and felt rage and an immense sadness sweeping through me. I thought it was utterly inhuman to send someone to tell me, in the precarious state I was in, that my future might be in jeopardy. The community acted without any thought for the harrowing experience I had just gone through. I had the feeling that my family was abandoning me a second time. I cried a lot.

But I hadn't seen anything yet. Shortly after the nun's visit, I received a parcel containing all my personal belongings: clothes, missal, holy pictures and passport, as well as a letter informing me that I could not go back to the community. In spite of the proof of my virginity, which I had furnished, the nuns remained convinced that the German soldiers had touched me sexually during my imprisonment. So I was impure and had to renounce my life as a bride of Christ. In fact, they made a request to Rome to release me from my vows.

This decision meant that the Red Cross had to take charge of me from now on because I no longer had a home in Europe. It also had to take care of my repatriation to Quebec.

I was humiliated and angry. I lost faith in Catholicism on that day and never regained it. I continued to believe in God and the Virgin Mary, but I've never set foot in a church again, except for a wedding or a funeral. I was outraged, and have borne a tremendous grudge ever since against anything religious. The Catholic Church treated me like a war criminal, banishing me from my community after I spent four years in captivity just because I happened to be in the wrong place at the wrong time. I was infuriated.

The only thing I felt like believing in right then was the solidarity among us, the girls with whom I'd lived through those years of horror. They had done more to help humanity than I would have as a nun. They hadn't needed to take vows in order to show kindness and sacrifice themselves for their neighbours. Thanks to them, I had survived. It was to this type of community that I wanted to devote myself from now on.

After a few weeks I finally calmed down, although I didn't forget the insult. I thought about my new situation, and all in all

I was content with my lot. I would be going home at last. I asked the people at the Red Cross if it might be possible for them to find my brothers in Quebec. Several weeks later they managed to get hold of the address of my brother Rosaire and sent him a telegram to let him know I was alive and well.

I wanted to start a new life, completely free to do what I pleased. No more constraints, no more isolation! To dress the way I felt like, eat what I felt like, to enjoy and savour life, my new life. Yes, it was going to be fantastic.

When I saw Léon walk into the room and being reunited with Simone after all that time, I knew what I wanted to experience. The two of them were such a lovely sight. They dissolved into tears while they kissed and I couldn't possibly say how long their embrace lasted. I, too, wanted to love and be loved.

For a while I thought about the rendezvous Franz had planned for us in Paris on May 7. But a ship had been chartered to repatriate Canadians. It was scheduled to leave in March of 1946. I knew I wouldn't have the means to come back to Europe.

Simone gave me her address in Brittany. Since she would have more opportunities to come to Quebec than I would to return to Europe, I told her I would write to her as soon as I arrived and give her my address. To our great delight we found Mathilde in another wing of our temporary hospital. The three of us spent several days talking. Simone and I thanked her from the bottom of our hearts for all she had done for us. She told us a bit about the "services" she'd had to perform in exchange for the privileges we enjoyed, which had saved our lives more than once. We felt that our thanks were quite feeble in comparison with what she had done.

Finally I said goodbye to them, assuring them they would forever have a huge place in my heart and not a day would go by without my thinking of them. We never saw Iréna again.

Coming Home

On March 4, 1946, at almost thirty-four years old, I boarded a Red Cross ship to return to Quebec. If I'd missed that opportunity, I would have had to work for several years to scrape together the fare for my return voyage. I will always be grateful to that organization.

The crossing lasted seven days. In the middle of the week, a storm began to rage and I was very scared. Massive waves crashed over the decks. The whole boat creaked and nearly all the passengers were ill. A foul odour pervaded the ship, mixed with a strong fuel-oil smell. I threw up more than once. It was as though the sea wanted to swallow us up, the boat feeling as light as an empty shell. We spent three days closeted in our cabins, waiting for the good weather to return.

Many of the passengers had been imprisoned in labour camps and were liberated at the same time as I was. We didn't mention it to each other, but we just knew. It showed. It was as though traces of dirt and humiliation still clung to our bodies. None of us had any desire to talk about our past experience.

By a strange coincidence I shared my cabin with three women. I had the same sense of security as with the girls at the camp.

We were all about the same age. Two were nurses with the Red Cross. The third had suffered a fate similar to mine, in a different camp. I quickly became friends with one of the two nurses, Gabrielle, whom I called Gaby. Her hair was auburn, like the colours of fall, and she had tiny freckles on her face. She seemed somewhat brash, but was, above all, a real fighter, having what it takes to overcome life's obstacles.

Until now, I had only met people on my path who helped me to forge ahead. I'm thinking of Sister Marguerite, Sister Adolphine, and the three girls at the camp. What would have become of me without them?

I was much less excited than on the journey that had taken me to Europe a few years earlier. I have to admit I had changed. I felt confused now. Four and a half years of imprisonment weighed on me, and I was bitterly disappointed to have been rejected by my congregation.

But something made up for this disappointment: I desperately wanted to live every moment of my new life to the full. I was going to meet up with my brothers again. I didn't know them well and that worried me. I wondered if Rosaire would be happy to see me. Would he want to put me up until I found a job and moved into a place of my own?

In the small suitcase the Red Cross had given me, I still had my nun's clothes. I didn't want to get rid of them before I received the letter from Rome that was supposed to confirm I was now a laywoman, in other words free, independent and … very much alone and practically homeless …

I spent a good part of the journey pondering my future. During the crossing's final days, Gaby, who knew nothing about my having been a nun — I was already ashamed to talk about it — told me things that made my hair stand on end. I had never heard a woman, or even a man, speak of such vulgar things. It went beyond basic sex education, which would have been kinder to my innocent ears.

Gaby went into great detail about her love affairs. As I

listened to her, I thought of what Mathilde had to endure for us all. She had no choice, I'm sure. It was a matter of survival.

The information would nonetheless be useful to me, I thought, because sooner or later I was bound to walk into a lion's den in the city of Montreal.

At the end of the voyage, Gaby gave me her mother's telephone number; she would be living with her for a while. She also suggested sharing an apartment as soon as I had a job. I leapt at the offer. She would definitely make it easier for me to survive in that urban jungle.

❖ ❖ ❖

The ship berthed in New York on March 11, 1946.

Gaby travelled with me on the train to Montreal and helped me find the address of my brother Rosaire.

My brother lived in a tiny apartment on rue Sainte-Élisabeth with his wife, Yvette. When I knocked on their door, I was very nervous. I had no idea what kind of welcome I would get. Rosaire was four when I last saw him. Would I recognize him? When he opened the door, we knew each other right away. We shed many tears before we could speak. I sensed in his embrace that nothing could separate us ever again. I felt a great rush of joy. I was now in the arms of someone of the same flesh and blood, who'd had the same parents, the same past. Rosaire didn't remember his childhood, but we had suffered the same tragedies, breathed in the same smells, lived in the same house. Recalling these details brought me tremendous comfort. I just couldn't stop looking at him. His features were familiar and I found him handsome. Rosaire was my younger brother. There were only two years between us, but I felt an urge to protect him. I thought I had finally met someone who would need me. In my heart and mind, he was still four years old.

He told me his life story, from the time when we were separated until the outbreak of the Second World War, in which he had fought in Europe. While, from a trench, he repelled an attack lasting several days, he caught pneumonia and was repatriated to Canada. He mentioned that one day, on a radio program where the list of people who died in the war was broadcast, he heard my name. He had burst into tears and had a mass said for me. I cheered him up by telling him this mass had surely helped me to survive. I asked him about Louis-Georges, who was just six months old when I left for the convent. He hadn't heard from him in ages. That was a pity because I would have very much liked to see him again.

I told Yvette and Rosaire almost everything — the convent, the religious life, my years at the camps, how I had been abandoned by my religious community — but I kept silent about the episode with Franz. I was ashamed of it now that the war was over. And doubly so because my brother had risked his life fighting the Nazis. I showed them my nun's habit and told them I would wait for the letter from Rome before getting rid of it. I spoke to them about the dressmaking trade I had learnt in those years. I wanted to look for work in that field. Yvette and Rosaire agreed to put me up in their small place until I could fend for myself.

After the war, everything had to be rebuilt. The economy began to grow again and I didn't have to look long for a job. Three days after arriving in Montreal, I was hired by a menswear factory. I made trouser pockets. It wasn't the quite the kind of sewing I would have liked to do, but I had to eat.

I called Gaby to let her know I was working and that in a month I would be able to share the expenses of the place she already had on rue Beaudry. It was an ideal location, not too far from my brother's home, only a minute away from rue Sainte-Catherine. The apartment had large windows and was therefore very bright. I felt a tremendous need for that light, as though I had to make up for all those years spent in darkness.

Gaby's mother had given her furniture, so the apartment was quite full. For several years Gaby had been assembling a trousseau but, being still single, she decided to use it. Her nurse's salary was more than enough for her to live on. She wanted for nothing.

As for me, I put a few pennies aside whenever I could in order to buy myself a sewing machine and fabric. On my days off I had fun making dresses, completely by hand. Gaby encouraged me. She said I had talent and should use it to earn my living. In the meantime I lived each day with passion.

Every Thursday, my meagre salary in my pocket, I went to treat myself to a pastry at Kresge's on rue Sainte-Catherine. As I bit into my napoleon, I thought of the camp and Simone in particular. I closed my eyes and inwardly called out to her so she might hear me in Brittany, "Here's to you, my guardian angel, and to our survival!" And when I bought a pattern to make an elegant dress, I would remember Mathilde. I had even renamed the hemstitch "Mathilde's stitch," because it's discreet but strong. That's how in my daily work I evoked the memory of the women who had done so much for me. It was my way of paying tribute to them. As for Iréna, I would pray every day until the end of my life that she might still be alive and had found true happiness.

On May 7, 1946, I thought of Franz constantly. Was he still alive? Had he gone to the place of our rendezvous? I don't think Germans were welcome in Paris at that time. Now that I was living a normal life again, my meeting with Franz had a completely different meaning. Such a love story was sheer madness even though I was no longer a nun.

A few months after my return, I received a letter from Rome releasing me from my vows. I was now officially free, like everyone else. I immediately destroyed my habit and hid all traces of my former life in a locked trunk. I had no regrets, but was still very angry with religion.

I lived these first weeks of my new-found freedom in a spirit of revolt. I felt like doing everything that used to be forbidden. I was thumbing my nose at the obedience I'd shown for all those years. It had been useless, after all.

Gaby, the red-haired demon, egged me on as I travelled down this rebellious road. It began by going to nightclubs, on weekends, where they put on shows. But it was also an opportunity to meet people. I loved nightlife, and luckily Gaby protected me against some wolves who were a bit too hungry. Yet it wasn't in those cabarets that I met the most wonderful gift of my life.

One evening, Gaby brought a man home. His name was Maurice. They had seen each other a few times at the hospital, where he came to visit his sister. Gaby was mad about him and had asked him over for a drink. Although I used to think that the expression "he is like a Greek god," when Gaby said it, might be an exaggeration, I felt it was almost too weak when I saw him. He could easily have been a movie star. Six feet two inches of elegance! He had freshly cut black hair, incredibly merry hazel eyes, hands I immediately fell for because they were broad and moved with ease. He wore a dark grey suit and his shoes glowed, having been polished to a mirror-like shine. But the ultimate weapon was his smile. I couldn't help looking at him. Although I was happy for Gaby that she had met such a man, I was jealous. It wasn't the kind of man I might have run into at work.

The three of us talked a lot and, without us being aware of it, Maurice noted our telephone number just before he left.

The following evening, when I answered the phone, I recognized his voice and told him Gaby wasn't home because she was working overtime at the hospital. "It isn't her I want to speak to, it's you," he said. I explained that Gaby would be angry with me if I agreed to go and have a Coke with him.

"I'm not interested in Gaby," he replied. "I think she is nice, but you are the one I would like to know better."

I accepted his invitation. We talked all evening. He still lived with his parents and was twenty-four years old. He had just landed a steady job at a sporting-goods warehouse. It's what he had been waiting for in order to leave the family home. He had done his military service late, having been conscripted. Fortunately, he hadn't had time to go and fight. His brother Robert wasn't so lucky. He died on the battlefields of Italy when he was just twenty-one, and now his two children were fatherless. His parents had found it very hard to come to terms with his death. Then, when it was my turn, I shared a slice of my life with him. He was captivated by my story. I didn't tell him everything, though. I kept silent about my time in the religious life and my feelings for Franz. That episode will remain forever secret.

Little by little, he cut Gaby out of his life. We went out together without her knowledge. The day Gaby found out what had been going on, she flew into an almighty rage. When I got home from work, I saw that she had put all my belongings on the balcony and the door was locked and bolted. I couldn't get in. She had left a note on my suitcase: "A fine friend you are!"

I felt like the lowest of the low. My best friend was devastated because of me, although Maurice had told her their relationship wouldn't go any further. I was unhappy. It was pointless to try and explain things because she was too angry with me. I took a taxi with my suitcase and boxes and went to my brother's home to tide me over until I found a new place to live. One week later I moved into a tiny, furnished one-bedroom apartment in Rosemont. Maurice stayed with me during the week and went to his parents on weekends.

He made his family believe it was more convenient for work-related reasons to rent a room in the city. His parents lived in Cartierville, a streetcar ride of over an hour from his workplace, morning and night. When the family found out we lived together, they considered us damned souls. We lived like this for eight years. In 1954, we decided to get married in front of witnesses. We had developed a very close relationship. It was as though existing on the fringe of society had made us stronger. We also had a perfect sexual harmony, joyful and unrestrained, which further strengthened our marriage ties.

With hindsight I must admit that Maurice didn't always have an easy life with me. He had to cope with the after-effects of my past. I still had this rage, buried deep inside, that would erupt into sudden fits of anger, often for no reason, and caused instant mood swings, whereas Maurice was always laughing. He was a fundamentally good man, who looked on the bright side of things. Even the weather never affected his disposition. If it rained, he found a way to keep himself busy indoors. When it was nice out, he planned his days accordingly. I admit this annoyed me sometimes. I wrongly thought that such a malleable nature might be a sign of weakness. How can I have made such a ridiculous judgment? For a long time I blamed myself for it, especially when all I had left to comfort me was his memory.

He often talked to me about his wish to have a child. Unfortunately, I couldn't give him what he wanted so badly because in the years I spent at the camp I had stopped having my period, with lasting consequences. Also, I was older than he was, and afraid I wouldn't have the patience to bring up a child.

In our first year of marriage, Maurice's sister became pregnant. It was an unwanted pregnancy. She was thirty-nine and still lived with her parents. She felt just as embarrassed about her condition as a teenager would have been. She knew I couldn't have children. So, before looking for total strangers, she asked us if we would agree to adopt the one she was carrying. Maurice was thrilled at the idea of bringing up a child with me, but rather than responding right away, he said he would think it over, and asked her not to do anything before he had given her his answer. He didn't force my hand. When I saw how happy he was, I immediately wanted to give him the great joy of being a parent. He was ecstatic, and I was happy, too, although a little fearful. Yet, with all I'd gone through in my childhood, I longed to have my own family.

Maurice's sister stayed in the countryside throughout her pregnancy to avoid gossip and so save the family's honour. During this time, Maurice and I prepared ourselves to give the child a proper home. We took our roles very seriously. We even found a notary who had the power to have the words "illegitimate child" removed from the register of baptisms. So when the child would read its birth certificate, there would be no trace of the adoption. This was vitally important to us.

On September 18, 1955, Maurice's sister gave birth to a beautiful baby girl.

That was you, dearest Lise! We had eagerly awaited the event. Before you were born, we often went to visit your mother in her refuge in the country. We were anxious to see your little face. When we did, I noticed you looked like Maurice, and in this resemblance I found your legitimacy. Everyone would say, "She's very much her father's daughter!" You have his eyes and you were a happy little girl, good-natured, very much like him.

Maurice just couldn't resist spending time with you. He played with you whenever he could. He was always down on the floor and you leaned on him constantly. The two of you were a great pair.

I have to tell you a secret: I was a bit jealous of all the attention Maurice gave you. Since you arrived, he only thought of you, only spent time with you, and you were very close to him. It seemed to me I was losing my relationship with him. Before you came, he was the only one I shared my time with. Now I had to share that time with you, as well. It must be because of the years I spent at the camps that I needed attention and affection so badly. I was like you: I wanted him to love me even more dearly and take me in his arms all the time. You had to stay at the orphanage for a few months, for administrative reasons, and that must be why you, too, needed a double dose of affection. But, in the end, the two of us learned to share our man.

When you were four, I was hospitalized to have a huge fibroid removed from my uterus. The tumour was so large it affected my kidneys. It was a direct result of my period having stopped in the camps.

The surgeon decided to remove everything, and, doing so, found cancerous cells in the kidneys. While you lay beside me in my hospital bed, I caught sight of the doctor as he talked to Maurice in the corridor. I saw Maurice cry for the first time. He paced up and down before coming back. He sat down close to me, put his head on my stomach, began to cry and said, "The doctor told me that at the rate the cancer is spreading, you may only have two years left to live." He used hints in that sentence so you wouldn't understand what it meant. Still crying, he added, "I won't be able to go on without you. I won't know how to bring up Lise by myself. I want to die before you."

We prayed every day with great fervour to the Virgin Mary. Six months later, blood tests showed no trace of malignant cells. This was one of the great pieces of news that have marked my life. I received a five-year respite, without any suffering. It lasted until June 18, 1965, to be more precise. I will curse that date until I die.

On that day I was thrown into turmoil yet again. We were coming back from doing our shopping, you and I. We pushed the door open, which, oddly enough, had been left ajar. Your father lay on the floor. I sent you to get help while I stayed with Maurice. I bathed his face with cold water and loosened his shirt. I kept shouting out his name. His eyes were rolled upwards and he moaned. I begged him to talk to me. Assistance was a long time coming. All of a sudden his skin turned blue. He hardly moaned at all now. I understood I was losing him. I held his head in my hands and screamed for help. It finally arrived. One person asked me not to stay there while they tried to resuscitate him.

I complied and sat down a little distance away. Everything was falling apart for me again, but this time adversity had won. I had no energy left to fight. My whole body said, "All right. I give up. The victory is yours ..." Maurice was only forty-three.

Then I lost track of time. People who were there that day have told me what happened next. Apparently I uttered sacrilegious curses and attacked God so violently they found it difficult to listen to me. A doctor prescribed tranquillizers, which I had to take during the three days of Maurice's viewing at the funeral home. I was in such despair I must have frightened the family.

They kept me so full of pills that I saw nothing of the ceremonies and I think it was actually better this way. My only regret, dearest Lise, and I apologize to you, is in those days of intense sorrow I completely forgot about you. I thank those who looked after you until I came down to earth.

After this difficult ordeal, we became closely knit. From then on, no one could drive us apart. I know you were afraid I would abandon you.

I hope that when you read these notebooks, you will understand the way I behaved now and then, which may have seemed unreasonable to you. Old wounds were in fact resurfacing at those times.

I thank you from the bottom of my heart for having been by my side. You enriched the rest of my existence, which might have been meaningless without you. Along with your father, you were the greatest gift life brought me. I will always love you.

Mom

Epilogue

If it's true that children choose their parents before coming into the world, Maurice and Armande would definitely have been my first choice.

Sharing my mother's life with you allowed me to learn many things about her, and myself as well.

I love her even more today.

One of my regrets is that she died shortly before you made it possible for me to earn a decent living thanks to the fine profession of humorist. I would have liked to spoil her and make her last days a little easier, but she died in poverty because at that time I myself had difficulty making ends meet. After her death, my career soared. Who knows if she wasn't behind me to help me forge ahead and make you laugh so that now *you* might adopt me?

While I wrote this book, I thought I sensed her presence. I had a feeling she laid her hands on mine when I wrote.

It was in May of 2004 that the idea of the book began to form and I started the research.

I wanted to share her life with you as a tribute to her and so she wouldn't have experienced all that suffering in vain. I fervently hope you have enjoyed her story and feel a tiny bit of compassion for her so that her soul receives a caress.

We all have our lot of suffering, but as I became familiar with her story, I realized I would never have survived such a tragedy. There's no question I would have given up long before.

It is important that young people know what really happened so it will never be forgotten.

My mother came to be an inspiration for me, which often helps me to start the day on the right foot.

Thank you, Armande.

Your daughter,
who wanted you
to become immortal.

Acknowledgements

My first thanks, which will never be adequate for the story she lived and passed on to me, go to my mother, Armande. To Ariane, with whom I began the extensive research the narration required, a big thank you.

My thanks also to Christiane for helping me put this extraordinary story in order.

And a huge thank you to the great Quebec author Chrystine, for sharing her knowledge with me, an amateur author.

I am grateful to Monique for her support and her assistance with a thorough examination of the narrative.

A truly special thanks to Valéry, the policewoman who gave me the chance to experience one of my life's great moments by arranging for me to meet a citizen from her district, Madame Iréna, who is Polish and Jewish and lived through all the horrors.

My immense gratitude goes to Madame Iréna, who told me the story of her life, which moved me deeply. I will always cherish her.

I want to thank Sister Éva Tremblay for putting into words a part of the puzzle that was missing from my story.

To the people at the Société historique du Saguenay a big thank you for giving me access to the treasures contained in their archives.

I am grateful to all those who decided to put their records on the Internet.

A warm thank you to Ève-Marie for contributing to my research with a document she gave me during one of my appearances on *Salut Bonjour*.

I am immeasurably grateful to Manon, Yvan, and Carole, who kept my life outside of my writing going by taking care of my affairs.

My thanks to Mado, who is part of my roots, for remaining my friend for life in spite of Armande's mood swings.

A triple thank you to my three dear Johannes. To the first, my long-time friend, for her great support. To the second, my angel of the Saguenay, who guides me in my life now and then because she knows the events that happened before my time. And finally to the Johanne who had faith in me and made my dream come true, the Johanne who made it possible for me to hold my mother's immortalized life story in my hands and smell the paper it is printed on, and with whom I shared all my weaknesses. I'll never be able to thank you enough.

To my right arm throughout the venture, who encouraged and supported me, who was by my side in my research, in my insecurity, my doubts, and especially in my cave away from the outside world: Thank you so much, Lorraine.

To Jacques, many thanks for turning me into a much less amateurish writer.

My gratitude to Karine, the extension of my memory.

To Daniel, who is involved in all my projects, my great supporter, my artistic rock, my coach, my agent, a big, sincere thank you.

And a thank you as huge as the sky to Claudie and Hugo, my children, who are larger than life and often more mature than I am. I'm proud of you and it's important to me that you be proud of me, too.

Thank you, my audience, for supporting me in my ventures and for all those years of loyalty. It gives me great joy to share the story of my mother's life with you.

Of Related Interest

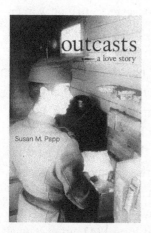

Outcasts
A Love Story
by Susan M. Papp
978-1554884223
$29.99

In this story of love and loss, Tibor Schroeder, a Christian and reservist in the Hungarian forces allied with Nazi Germany, and Hedy Weisz, a young Jewish woman, meet and fall in love during the Second World War — a time when romantic liaisons and marriage between Christians and Jews were not only frowned upon, but against the law. Not knowing of the dangers that await them, Tibor and Hedy pledge their lives to each only to be torn apart when Hedy and her family are herded into one Nagyszollos' ghettoes. Twenty-five years pass before the lovers are finally reunited in Canada. Based on true events.

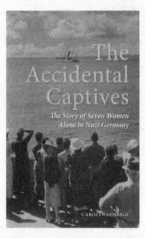